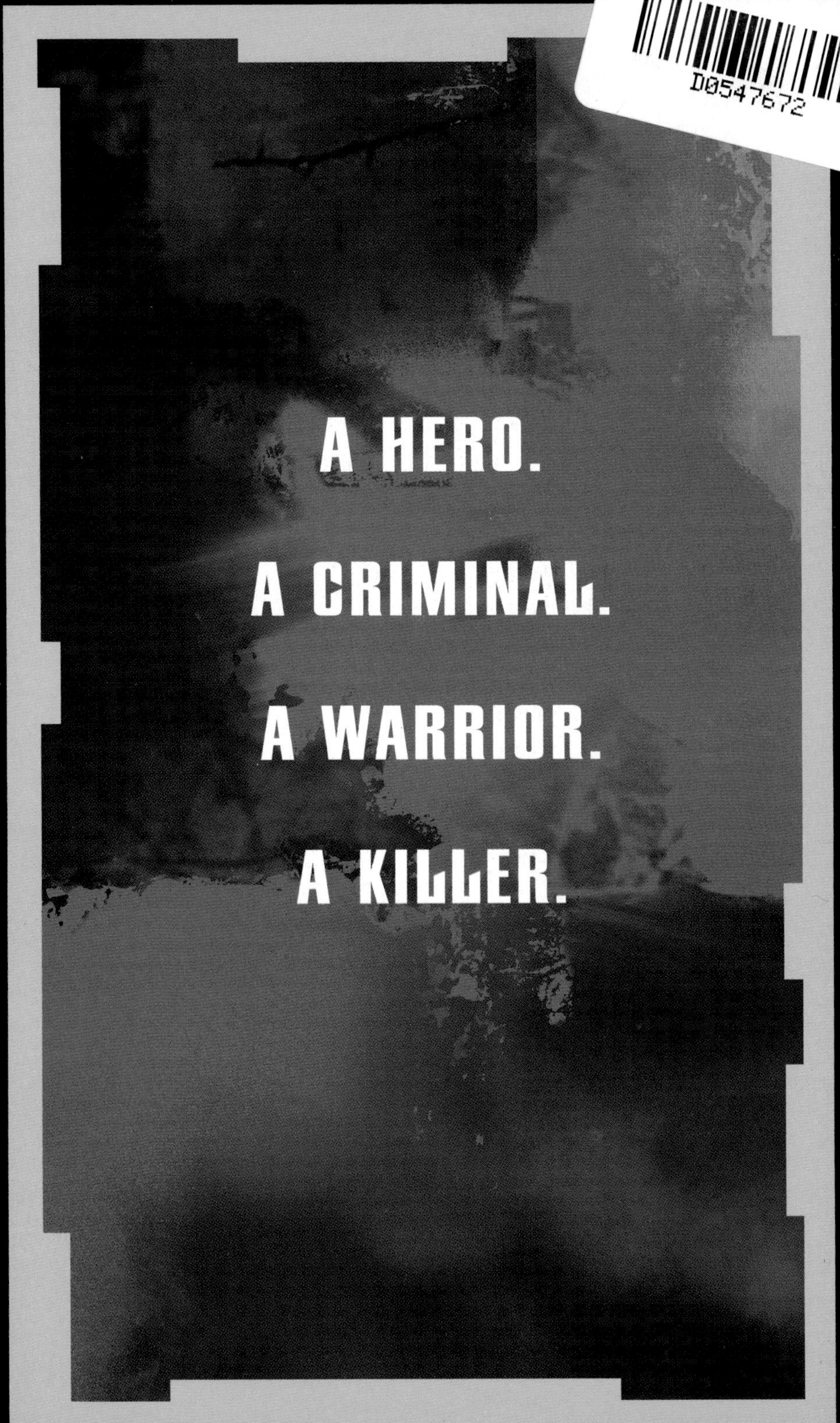

A HERO.

A CRIMINAL.

A WARRIOR.

A KILLER.

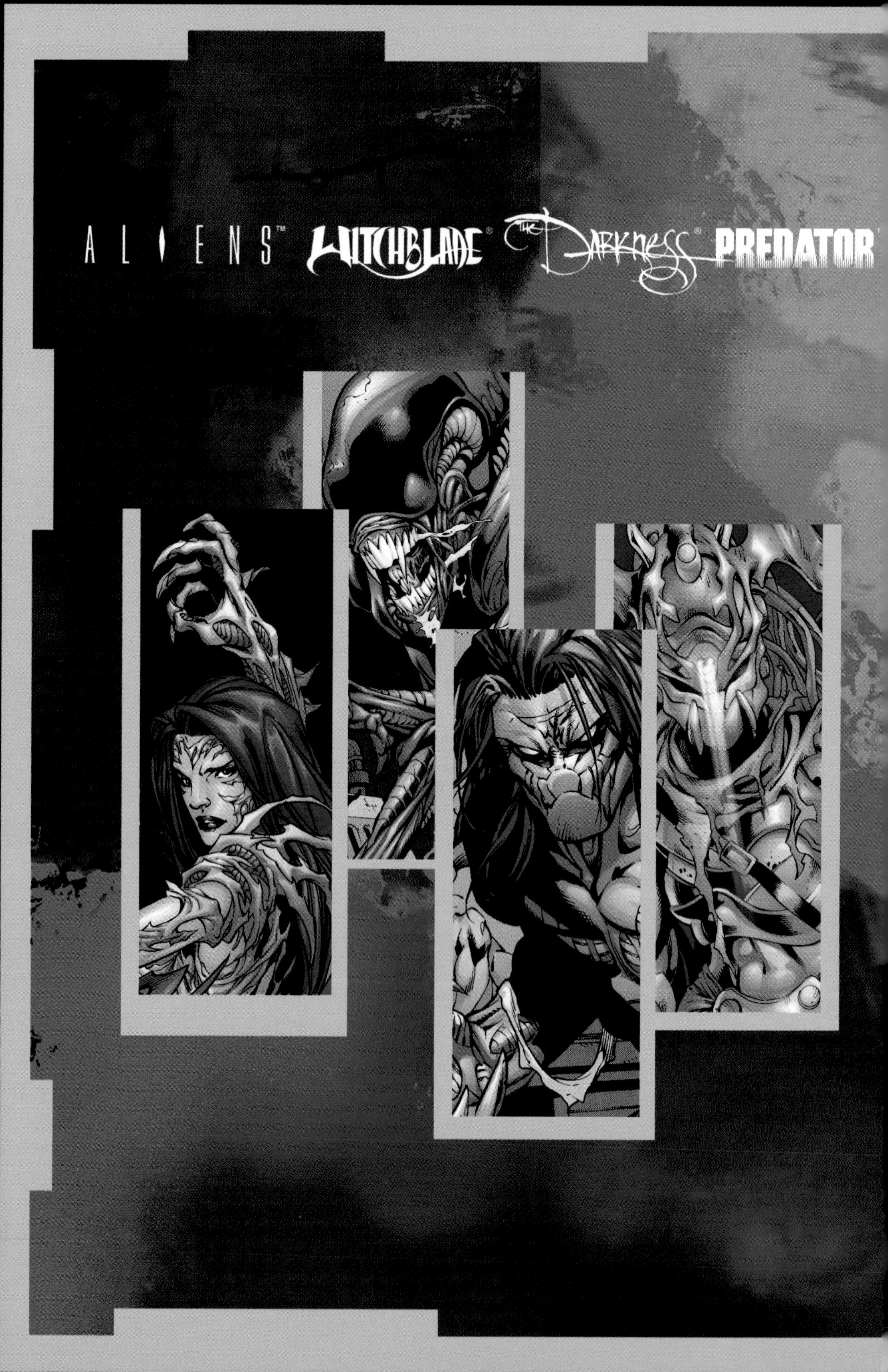
ALIENS WITCHBLADE THE DARKNESS PREDATOR

MINDHUNTER™

WRITER
DAVID QUINN

PENCILS
MEL RUBI

INKS
MIKE PERKINS

COLORS
DAN JACKSON

LETTERING
CLEM ROBINS

COVER
ERIC KOHLER

DARK HORSE COMICS® / TOP COW PRODUCTIONS, INC.®

ORIGINAL SERIES COVERS
DWAYNE TURNER

ASSISTANT EDITORS
TIM ERVIN-GORE & PHILIP SIMON

EDITOR
PHIL AMARA

DESIGNER
JEREMY PERKINS

PUBLISHER
MIKE RICHARDSON

MINDHUNTER: ALIENS-WITCHBLADE-DARKNESS-PREDATOR

Special thanks to Debbie Olshan at Fox, and Sonia Im, Jason Ross,
Renae Geerlings, and Matt Hawkins at Top Cow.

published by
Dark Horse Comics, Inc.
10956 S.E. Main Street
Milwaukie, OR 97222

www.darkhorse.com

To find a comics shop in your area,
call the Comic Shop Locator Service
toll-free at 1-888-266-4226

First edition: August 2001
ISBN: 1-56971-615-3

1 3 5 7 9 10 8 6 4 2

Printed in Singapore

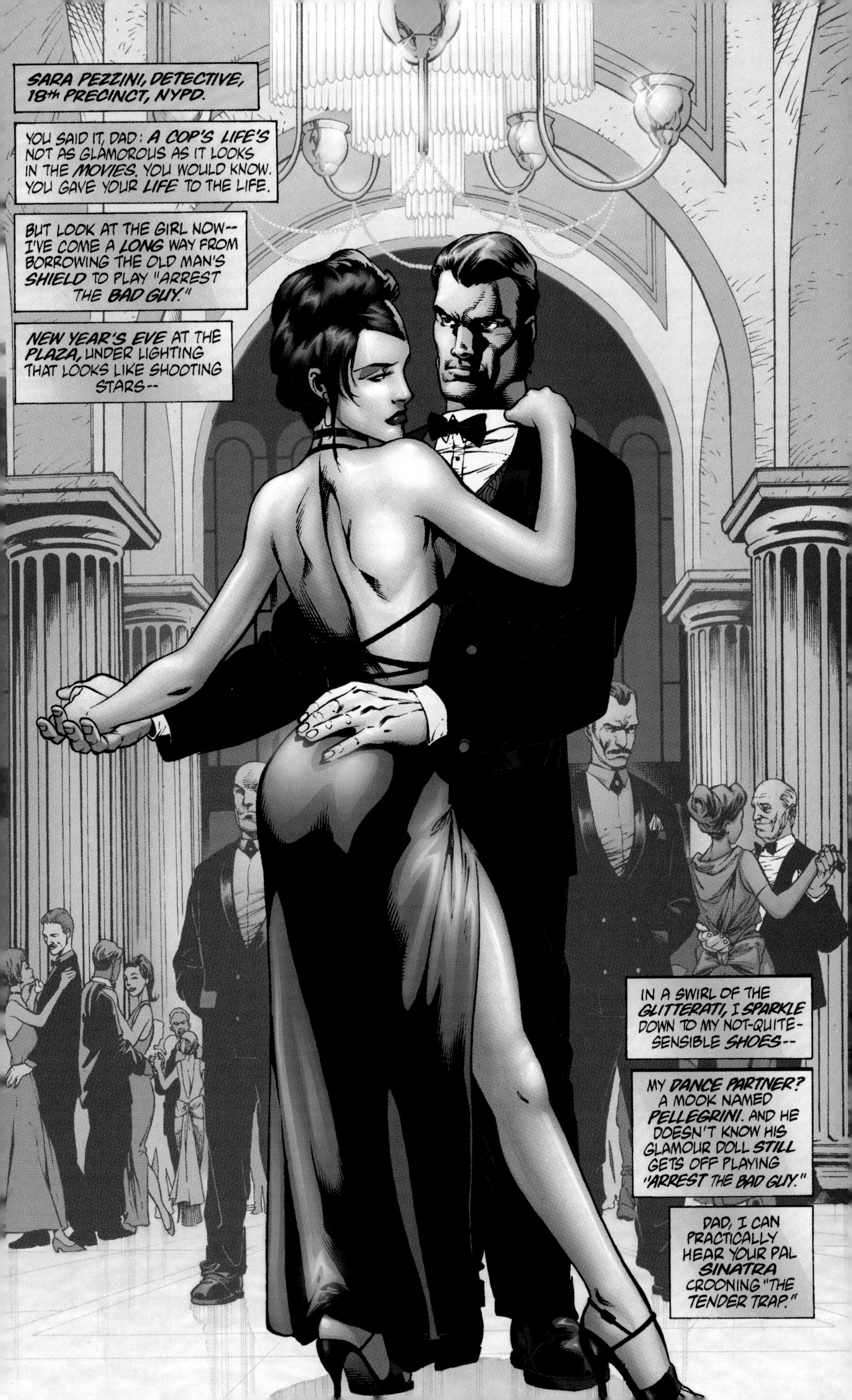
SARA PEZZINI, DETECTIVE, 18th PRECINCT, NYPD.
YOU SAID IT, DAD: A COP'S LIFE'S NOT AS GLAMOROUS AS IT LOOKS IN THE MOVIES. YOU WOULD KNOW. YOU GAVE YOUR LIFE TO THE LIFE.
BUT LOOK AT THE GIRL NOW-- I'VE COME A LONG WAY FROM BORROWING THE OLD MAN'S SHIELD TO PLAY "ARREST THE BAD GUY."
NEW YEAR'S EVE AT THE PLAZA, UNDER LIGHTING THAT LOOKS LIKE SHOOTING STARS--
IN A SWIRL OF THE GLITTERATI, I SPARKLE DOWN TO MY NOT-QUITE-SENSIBLE SHOES--
MY DANCE PARTNER? A MOOK NAMED PELLEGRINI. AND HE DOESN'T KNOW HIS GLAMOUR DOLL STILL GETS OFF PLAYING "ARREST THE BAD GUY."
DAD, I CAN PRACTICALLY HEAR YOUR PAL SINATRA CROONING "THE TENDER TRAP."

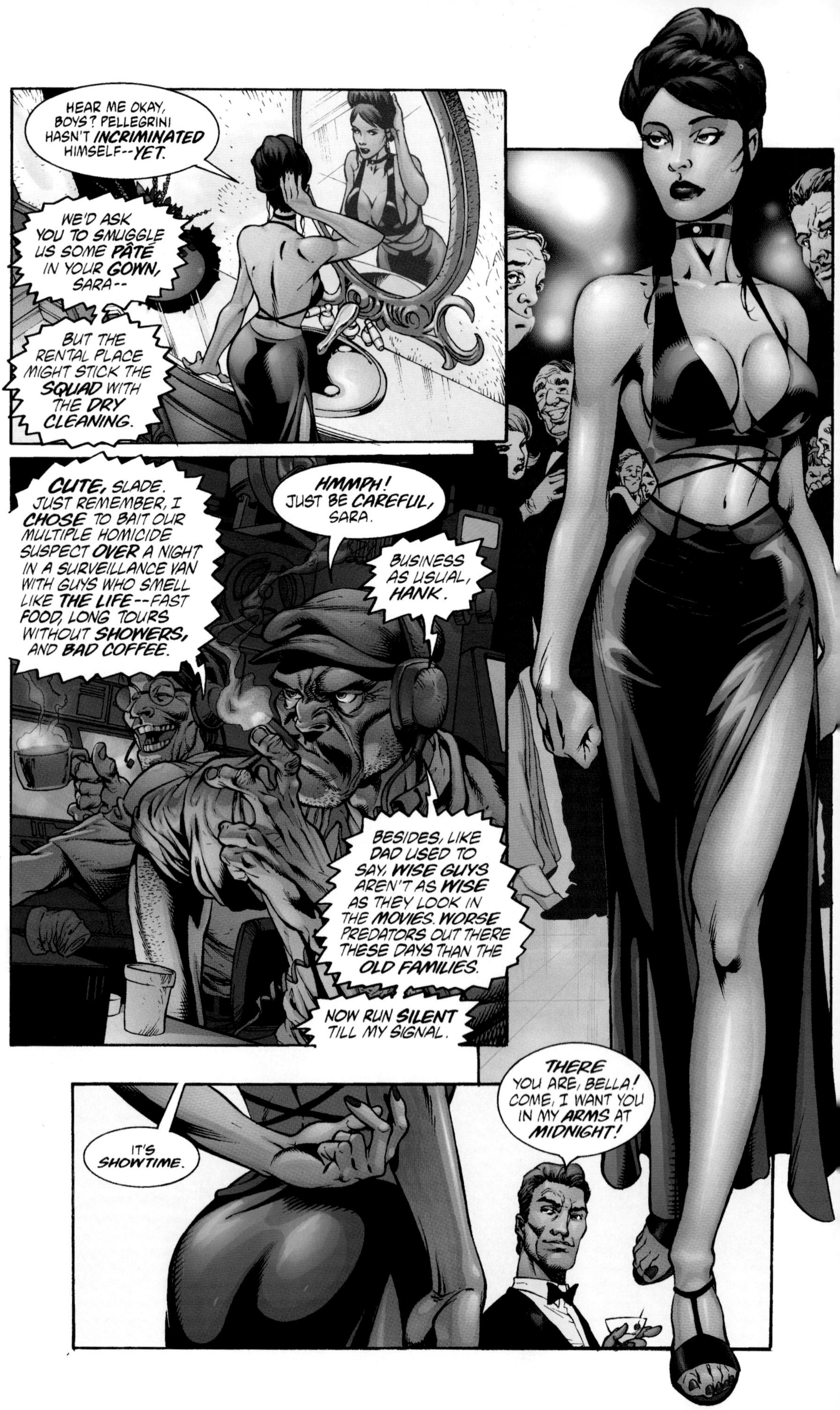
HEAR ME OKAY, BOYS? PELLEGRINI HASN'T INCRIMINATED HIMSELF--YET.
WE'D ASK YOU TO SMUGGLE US SOME PÂTÉ IN YOUR GOWN, SARA--
BUT THE RENTAL PLACE MIGHT STICK THE SQUAD WITH THE DRY CLEANING.
CUTE, SLADE. JUST REMEMBER, I CHOSE TO BAIT OUR MULTIPLE HOMICIDE SUSPECT OVER A NIGHT IN A SURVEILLANCE VAN WITH GUYS WHO SMELL LIKE THE LIFE--FAST FOOD, LONG TOURS WITHOUT SHOWERS, AND BAD COFFEE.
HMMPH! JUST BE CAREFUL, SARA.
BUSINESS AS USUAL, HANK.
BESIDES, LIKE DAD USED TO SAY, WISE GUYS AREN'T AS WISE AS THEY LOOK IN THE MOVIES. WORSE PREDATORS OUT THERE THESE DAYS THAN THE OLD FAMILIES.
NOW RUN SILENT TILL MY SIGNAL.
IT'S SHOWTIME.
THERE YOU ARE, BELLA! COME, I WANT YOU IN MY ARMS AT MIDNIGHT!

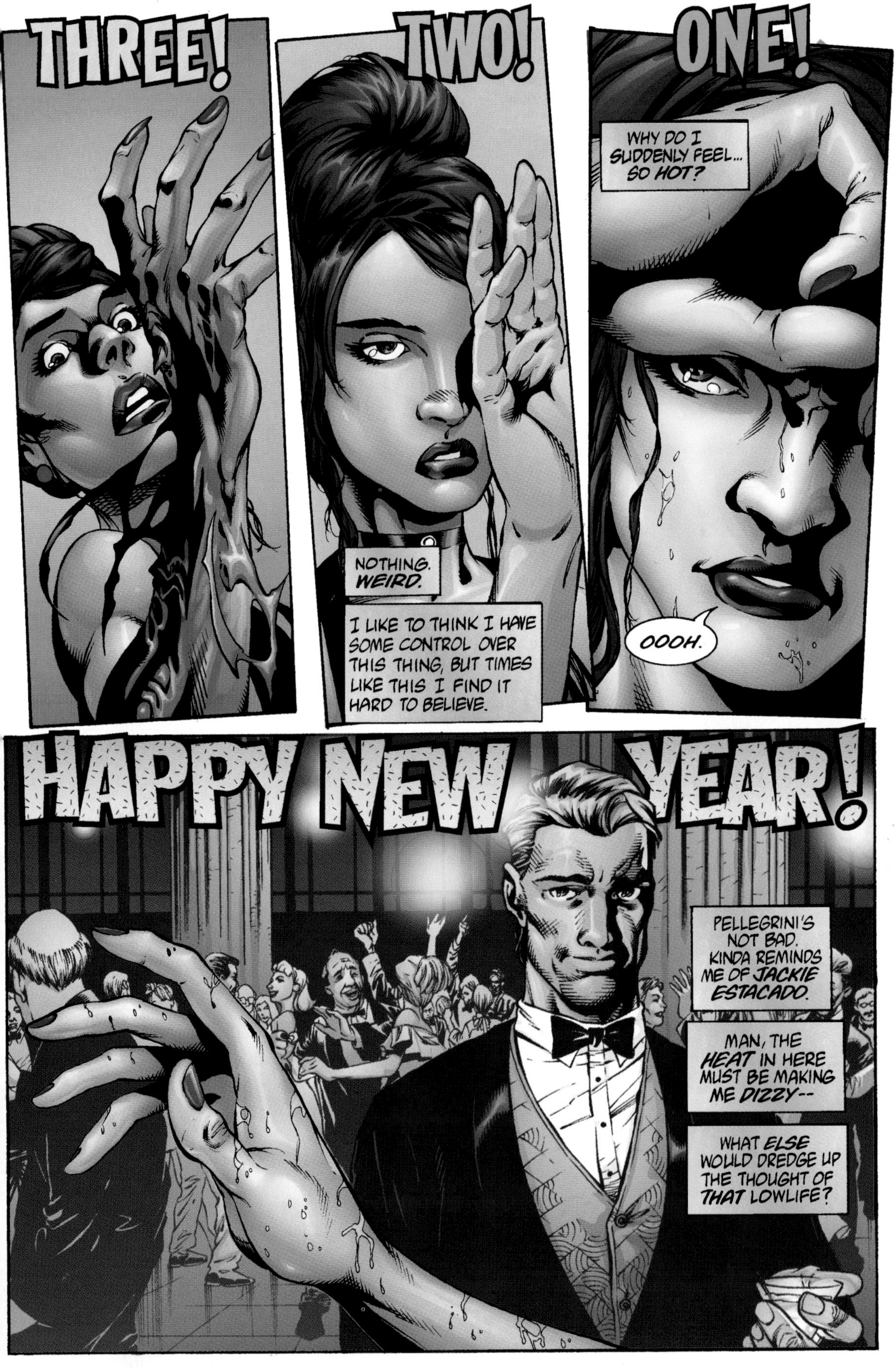
THREE!
TWO!
NOTHING. WEIRD.
I LIKE TO THINK I HAVE SOME CONTROL OVER THIS THING, BUT TIMES LIKE THIS I FIND IT HARD TO BELIEVE.
ONE!
WHY DO I SUDDENLY FEEL... SO HOT?
OOOH.
HAPPY NEW YEAR!
PELLEGRINI'S NOT BAD. KINDA REMINDS ME OF JACKIE ESTACADO.
MAN, THE HEAT IN HERE MUST BE MAKING ME DIZZY--
WHAT ELSE WOULD DREDGE UP THE THOUGHT OF THAT LOWLIFE?

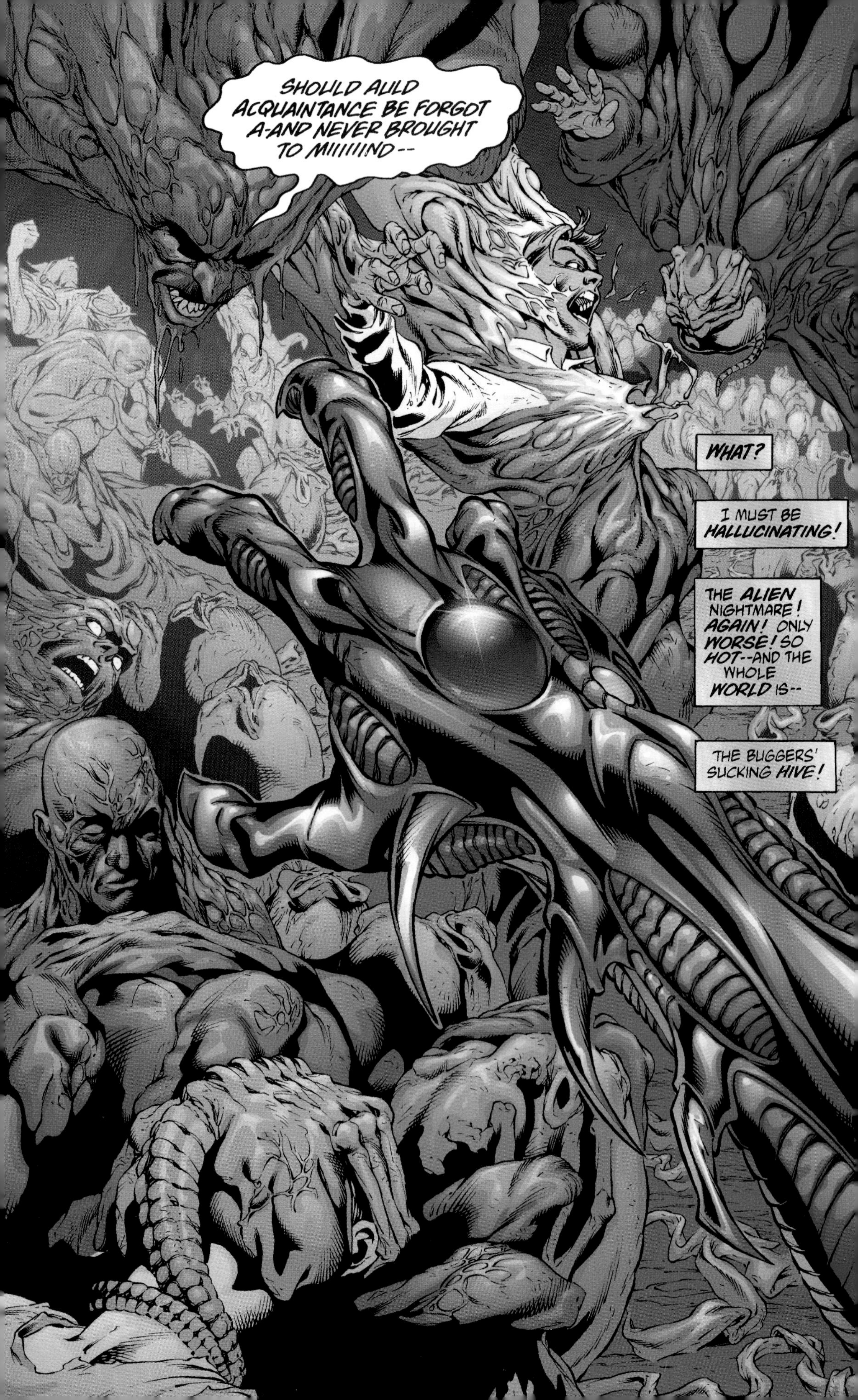
SHOULD AULD ACQUAINTANCE BE FORGOT A-AND NEVER BROUGHT TO MIIIIIIND--
WHAT?
I MUST BE HALLUCINATING!
THE ALIEN NIGHTMARE! AGAIN! ONLY WORSE! SO HOT--AND THE WHOLE WORLD IS--
THE BUGGERS' SUCKING HIVE!

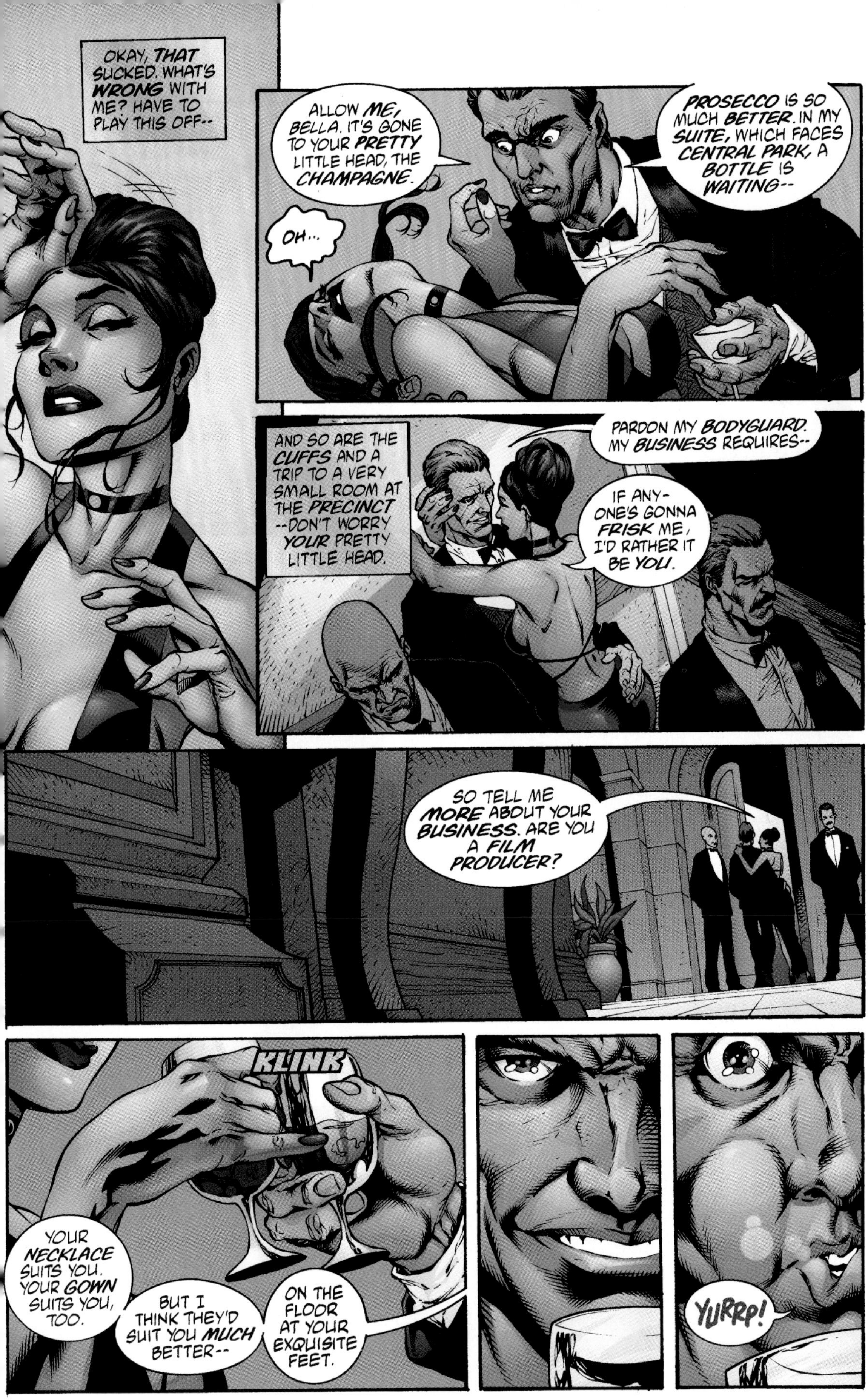
OKAY, THAT SUCKED. WHAT'S WRONG WITH ME? HAVE TO PLAY THIS OFF--
ALLOW ME, BELLA. IT'S GONE TO YOUR PRETTY LITTLE HEAD, THE CHAMPAGNE.
OH...
PROSECCO IS SO MUCH BETTER. IN MY SUITE, WHICH FACES CENTRAL PARK, A BOTTLE IS WAITING--
AND SO ARE THE CUFFS AND A TRIP TO A VERY SMALL ROOM AT THE PRECINCT --DON'T WORRY YOUR PRETTY LITTLE HEAD.
PARDON MY BODYGUARD. MY BUSINESS REQUIRES--
IF ANY-ONE'S GONNA FRISK ME, I'D RATHER IT BE YOU.
SO TELL ME MORE ABOUT YOUR BUSINESS. ARE YOU A FILM PRODUCER?
KLINK
YOUR NECKLACE SUITS YOU. YOUR GOWN SUITS YOU, TOO.
BUT I THINK THEY'D SUIT YOU MUCH BETTER--
ON THE FLOOR AT YOUR EXQUISITE FEET.
YURRP!

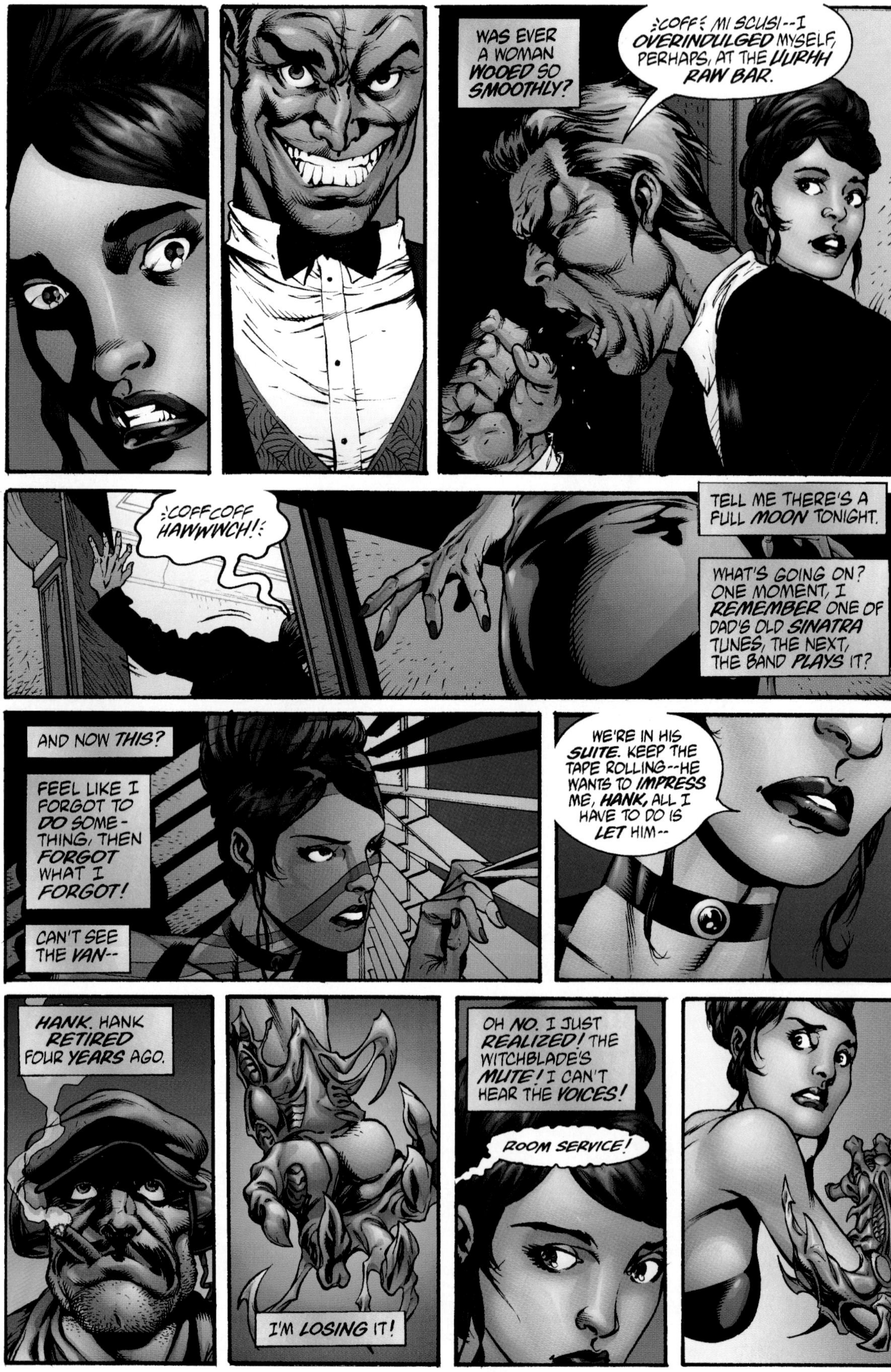
WAS EVER A WOMAN WOOED SO SMOOTHLY?
COFF MI SCUSI--I OVERINDULGED MYSELF, PERHAPS, AT THE UURHH RAW BAR.
COFFCOFF HAWWWCH!
TELL ME THERE'S A FULL MOON TONIGHT.
WHAT'S GOING ON? ONE MOMENT, I REMEMBER ONE OF DAD'S OLD SINATRA TUNES, THE NEXT, THE BAND PLAYS IT?
AND NOW THIS?
FEEL LIKE I FORGOT TO DO SOME-THING, THEN FORGOT WHAT I FORGOT!
CAN'T SEE THE VAN--
WE'RE IN HIS SUITE. KEEP THE TAPE ROLLING--HE WANTS TO IMPRESS ME, HANK, ALL I HAVE TO DO IS LET HIM--
HANK. HANK RETIRED FOUR YEARS AGO.
I'M LOSING IT!
OH NO. I JUST REALIZED! THE WITCHBLADE'S MUTE! I CAN'T HEAR THE VOICES!
ROOM SERVICE!

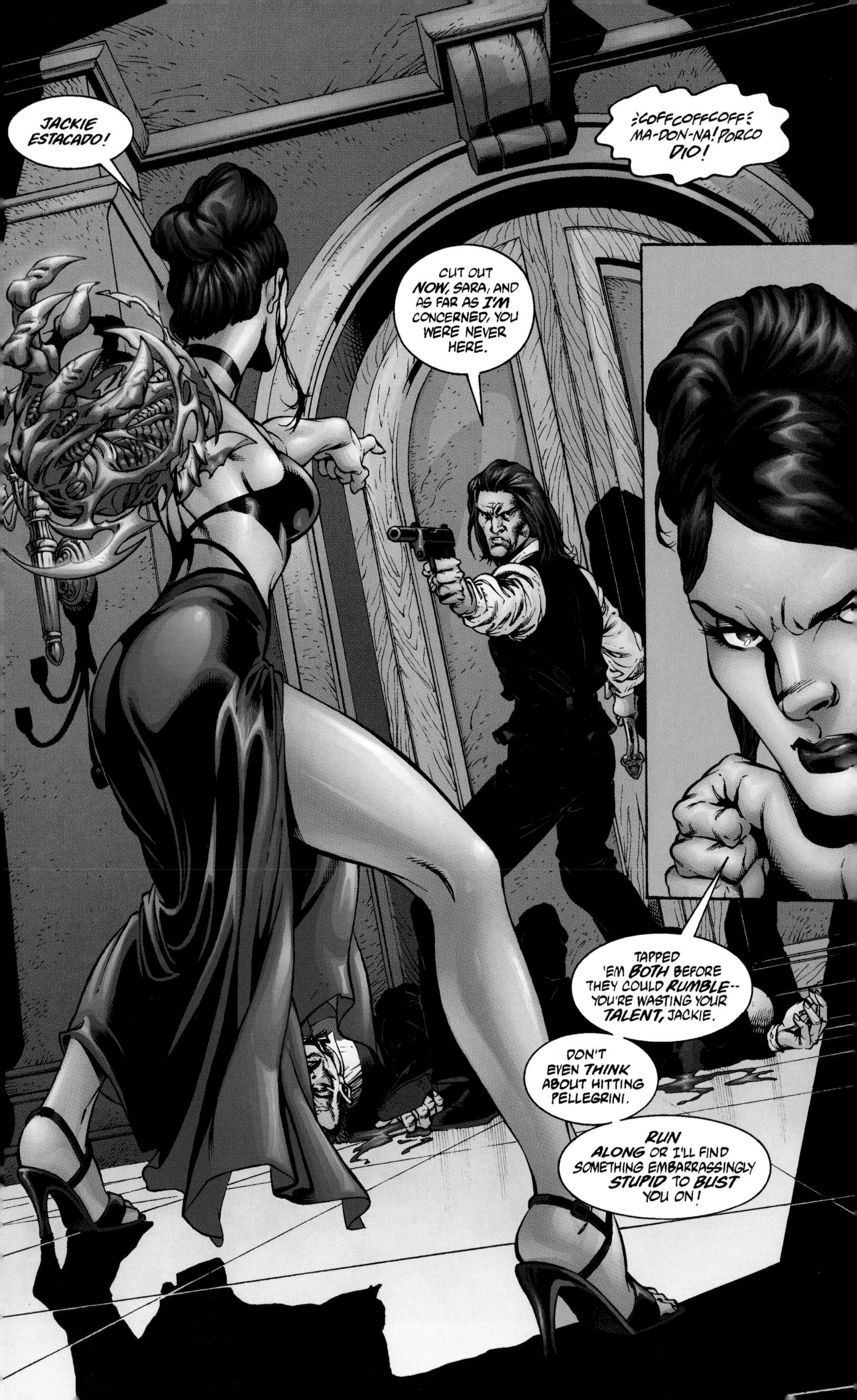
JACKIE ESTACADO!
:COFFCOFFCOFF: MA-DON-NA! PORCO DIO!
CUT OUT NOW, SARA, AND AS FAR AS I'M CONCERNED, YOU WERE NEVER HERE.
TAPPED 'EM BOTH BEFORE THEY COULD RUMBLE-- YOU'RE WASTING YOUR TALENT, JACKIE.
DON'T EVEN THINK ABOUT HITTING PELLEGRINI.
RUN ALONG OR I'LL FIND SOMETHING EMBARRASSINGLY STUPID TO BUST YOU ON!

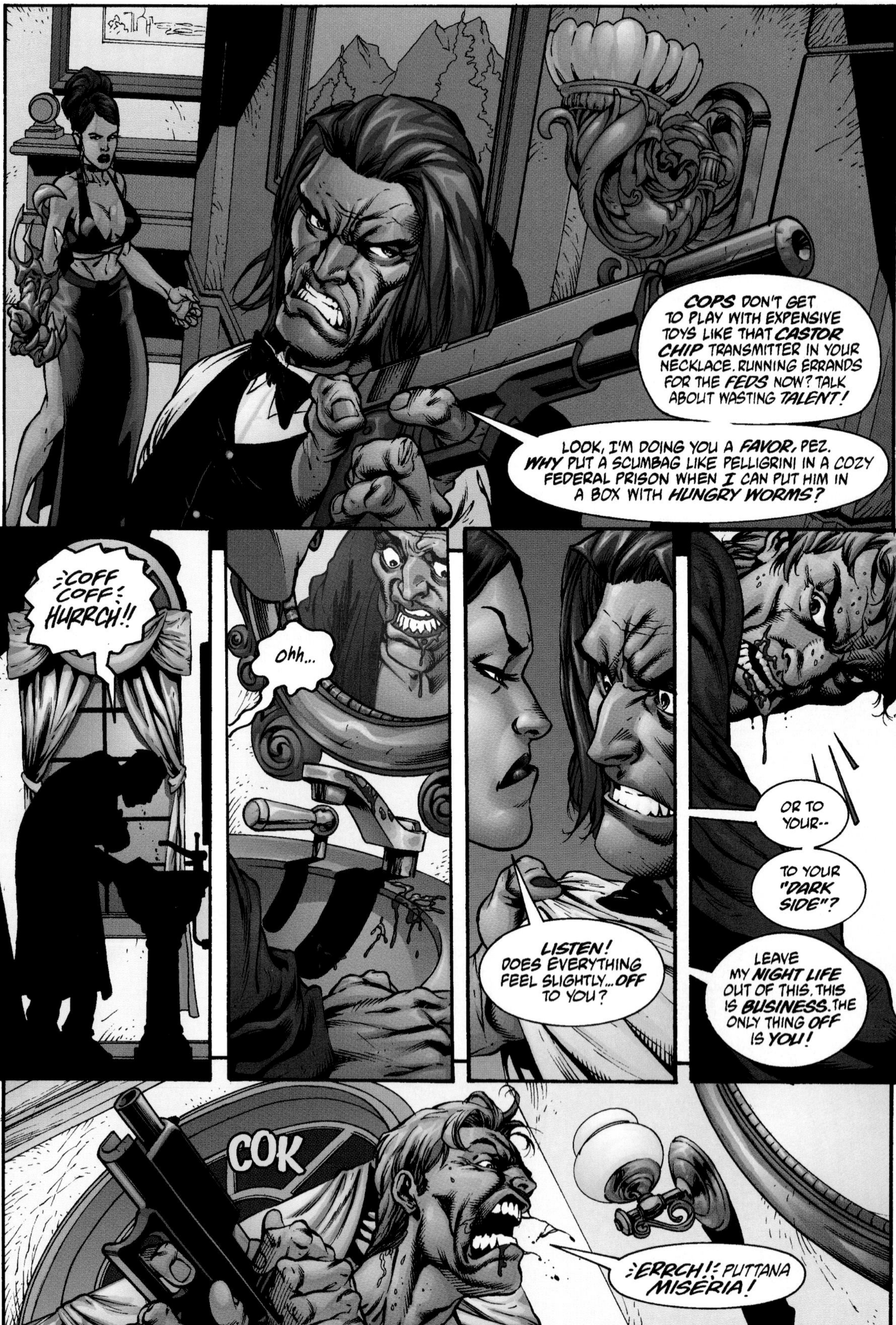
COPS DON'T GET TO PLAY WITH EXPENSIVE TOYS LIKE THAT CASTOR CHIP TRANSMITTER IN YOUR NECKLACE. RUNNING ERRANDS FOR THE FEDS NOW? TALK ABOUT WASTING TALENT!
LOOK, I'M DOING YOU A FAVOR, PEZ. WHY PUT A SCUMBAG LIKE PELLIGRINI IN A COZY FEDERAL PRISON WHEN I CAN PUT HIM IN A BOX WITH HUNGRY WORMS?
COFF COFF HURRCH!!
Ohh...
LISTEN! DOES EVERYTHING FEEL SLIGHTLY...OFF TO YOU?
OR TO YOUR--
TO YOUR "DARK SIDE"?
LEAVE MY NIGHT LIFE OUT OF THIS. THIS IS BUSINESS. THE ONLY THING OFF IS YOU!
COK
ERRCH! PUTTANA MISÈRIA!

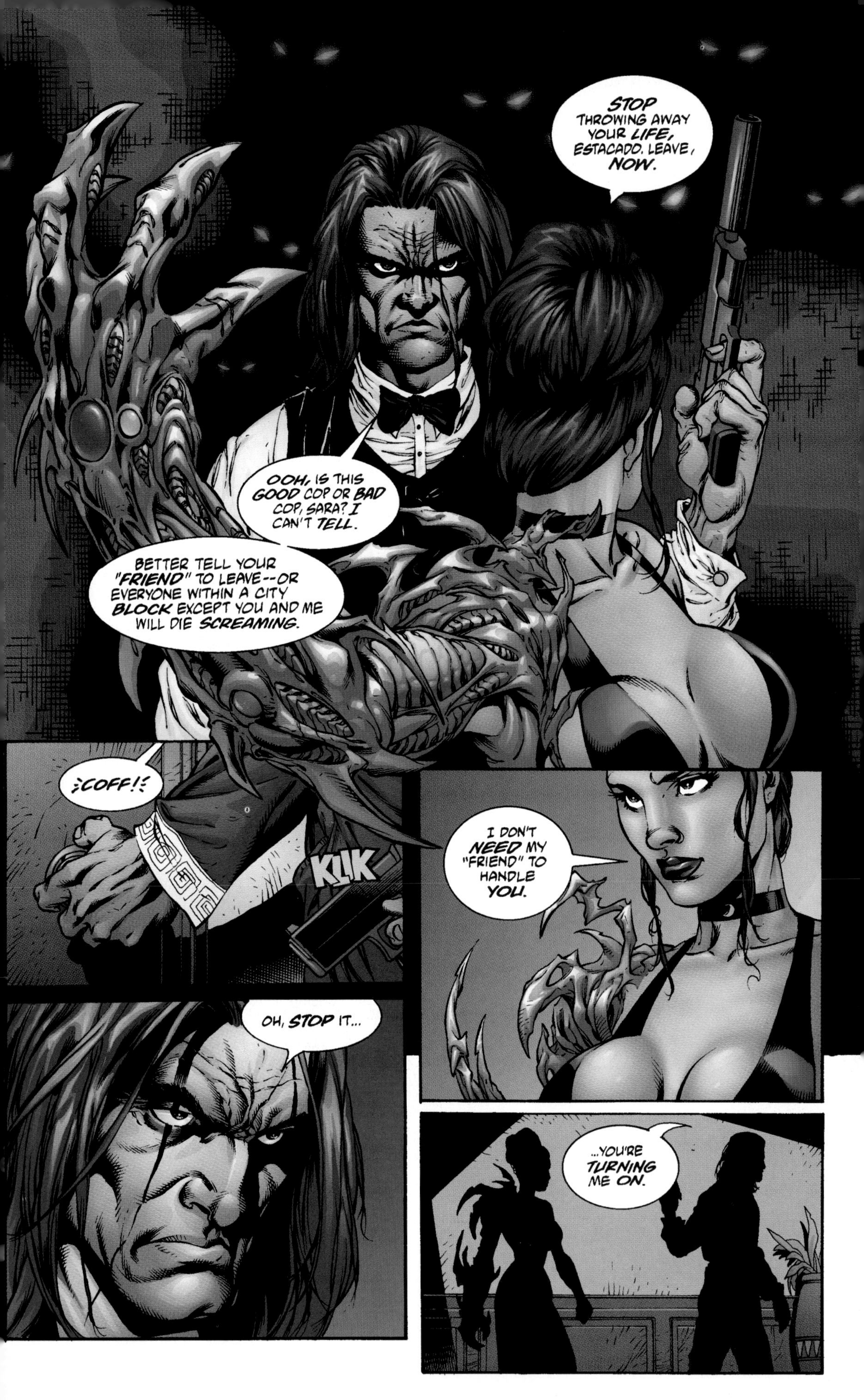
STOP THROWING AWAY YOUR LIFE, ESTACADO. LEAVE, NOW.
OOH, IS THIS GOOD COP OR BAD COP, SARA? I CAN'T TELL.
BETTER TELL YOUR "FRIEND" TO LEAVE--OR EVERYONE WITHIN A CITY BLOCK EXCEPT YOU AND ME WILL DIE SCREAMING.
¡COFF!¡
KLIK
I DON'T NEED MY "FRIEND" TO HANDLE YOU.
OH, STOP IT...
...YOU'RE TURNING ME ON.

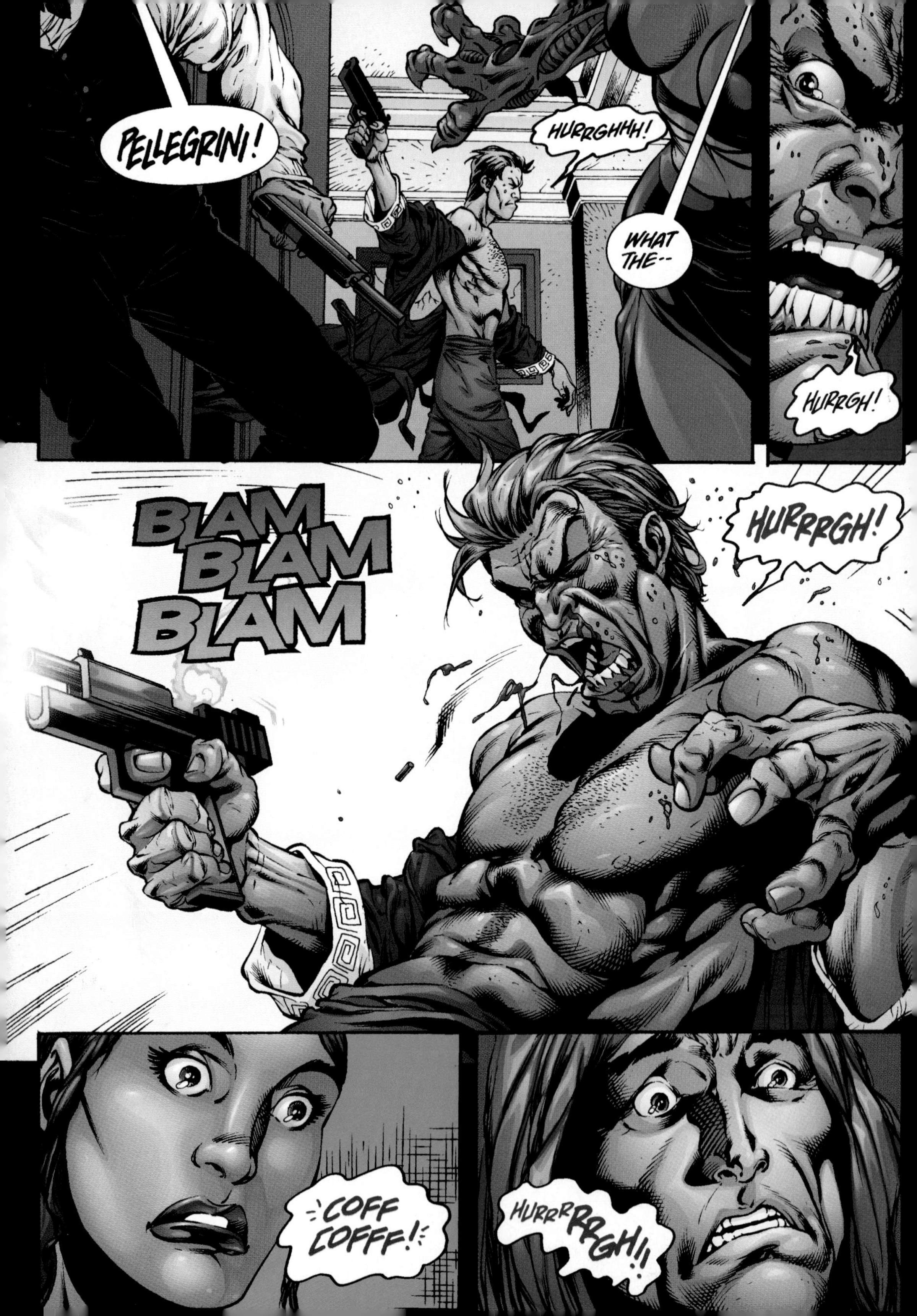
PELLEGRINI!
HURRGHHH!
WHAT THE--
HURRGH!
BLAM BLAM BLAM
HURRRGH!
COFF COFFF!
HURRRRRGH!!

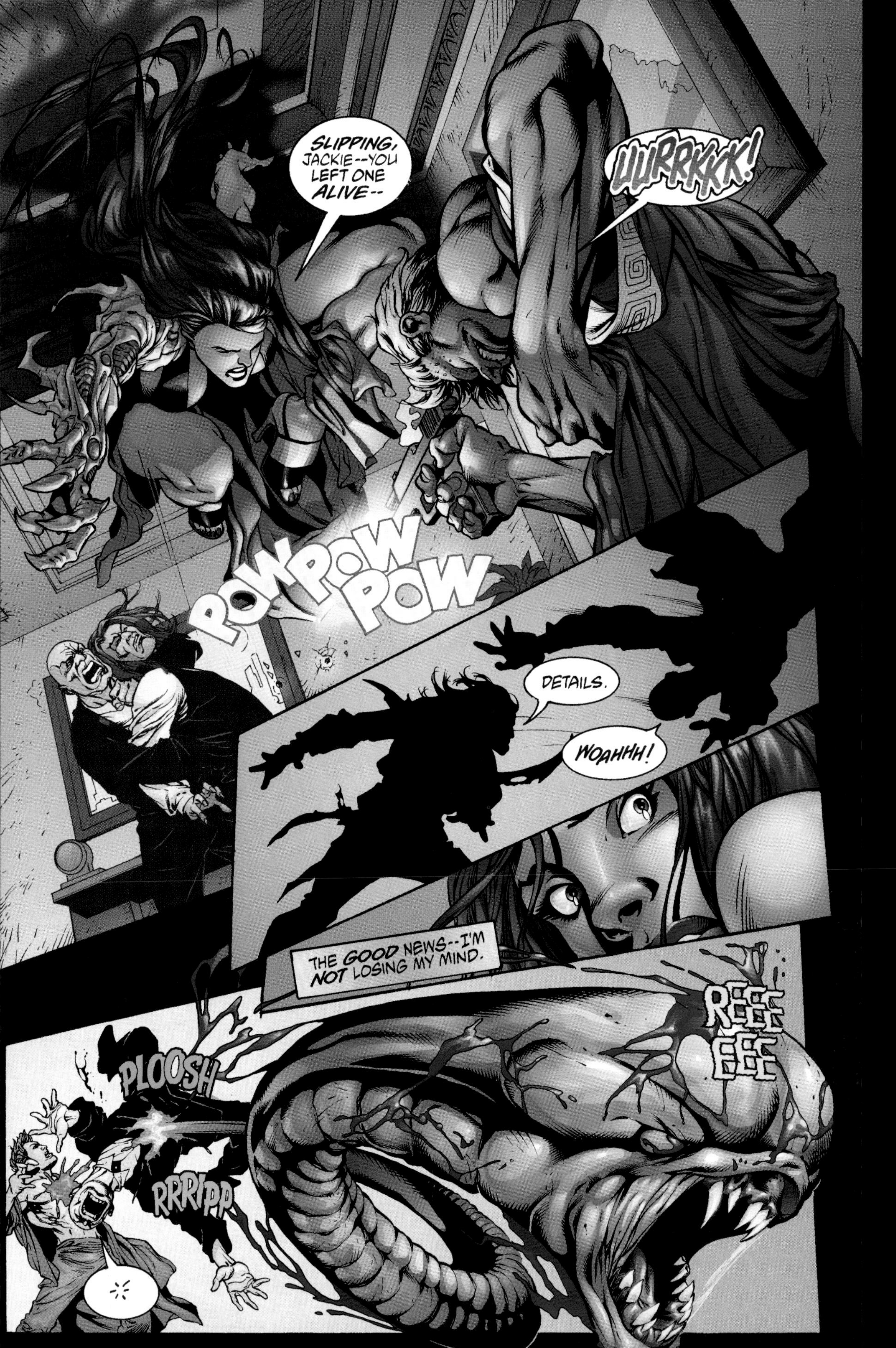
SLIPPING, JACKIE--YOU LEFT ONE ALIVE--
UURRKKK!
POW POW POW
DETAILS.
WOAHHH!
THE GOOD NEWS--I'M NOT LOSING MY MIND.
PLOOSH
REEE EEE
RRRIPP

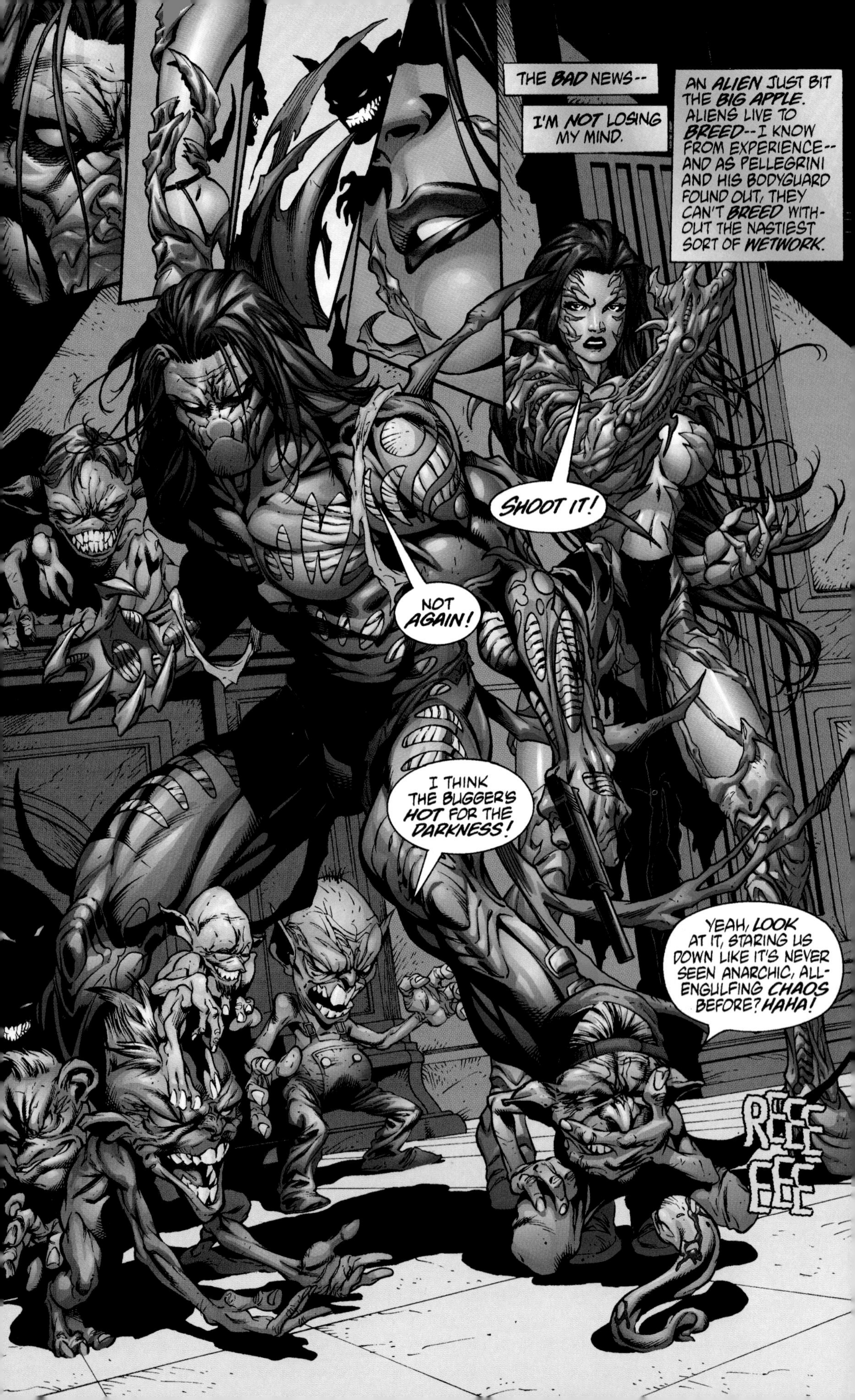
THE BAD NEWS--
I'M NOT LOSING MY MIND.
AN ALIEN JUST BIT THE BIG APPLE. ALIENS LIVE TO BREED--I KNOW FROM EXPERIENCE--AND AS PELLEGRINI AND HIS BODYGUARD FOUND OUT, THEY CAN'T BREED WITH-OUT THE NASTIEST SORT OF WETWORK.
SHOOT IT!
NOT AGAIN!
I THINK THE BUGGER'S HOT FOR THE DARKNESS!
YEAH, LOOK AT IT, STARING US DOWN LIKE IT'S NEVER SEEN ANARCHIC, ALL-ENGULFING CHAOS BEFORE? HAHA!
REEE EEE

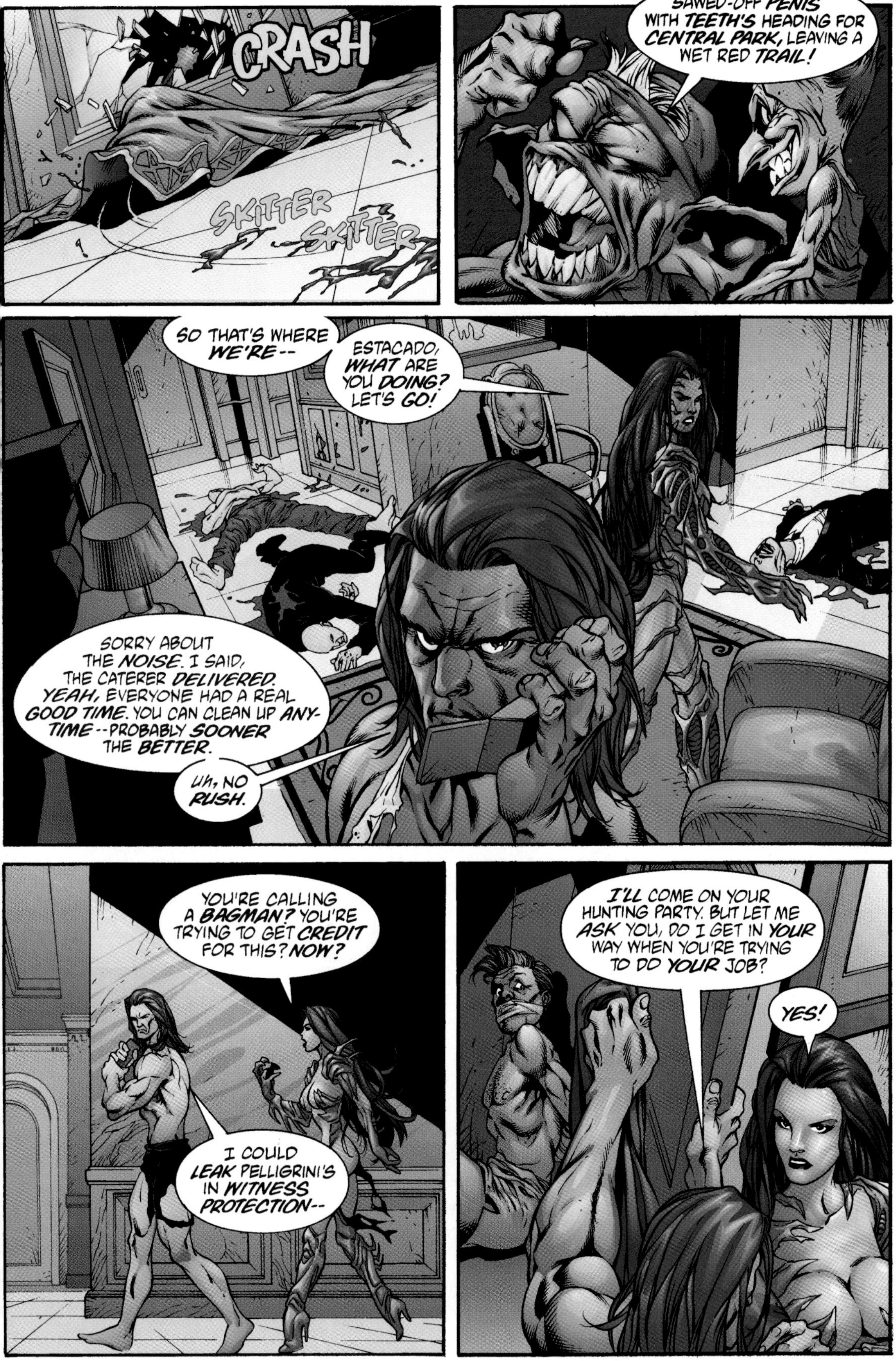
CRASH
SKITTER SKITTER
SAWED-OFF PENIS WITH TEETH'S HEADING FOR CENTRAL PARK, LEAVING A WET RED TRAIL!
SO THAT'S WHERE WE'RE--
ESTACADO, WHAT ARE YOU DOING? LET'S GO!
SORRY ABOUT THE NOISE. I SAID, THE CATERER DELIVERED. YEAH, EVERYONE HAD A REAL GOOD TIME. YOU CAN CLEAN UP ANY-TIME--PROBABLY SOONER THE BETTER.
UH, NO RUSH.
YOU'RE CALLING A BAGMAN? YOU'RE TRYING TO GET CREDIT FOR THIS? NOW?
I COULD LEAK PELLIGRINI'S IN WITNESS PROTECTION--
I'LL COME ON YOUR HUNTING PARTY. BUT LET ME ASK YOU, DO I GET IN YOUR WAY WHEN YOU'RE TRYING TO DO YOUR JOB?
YES!

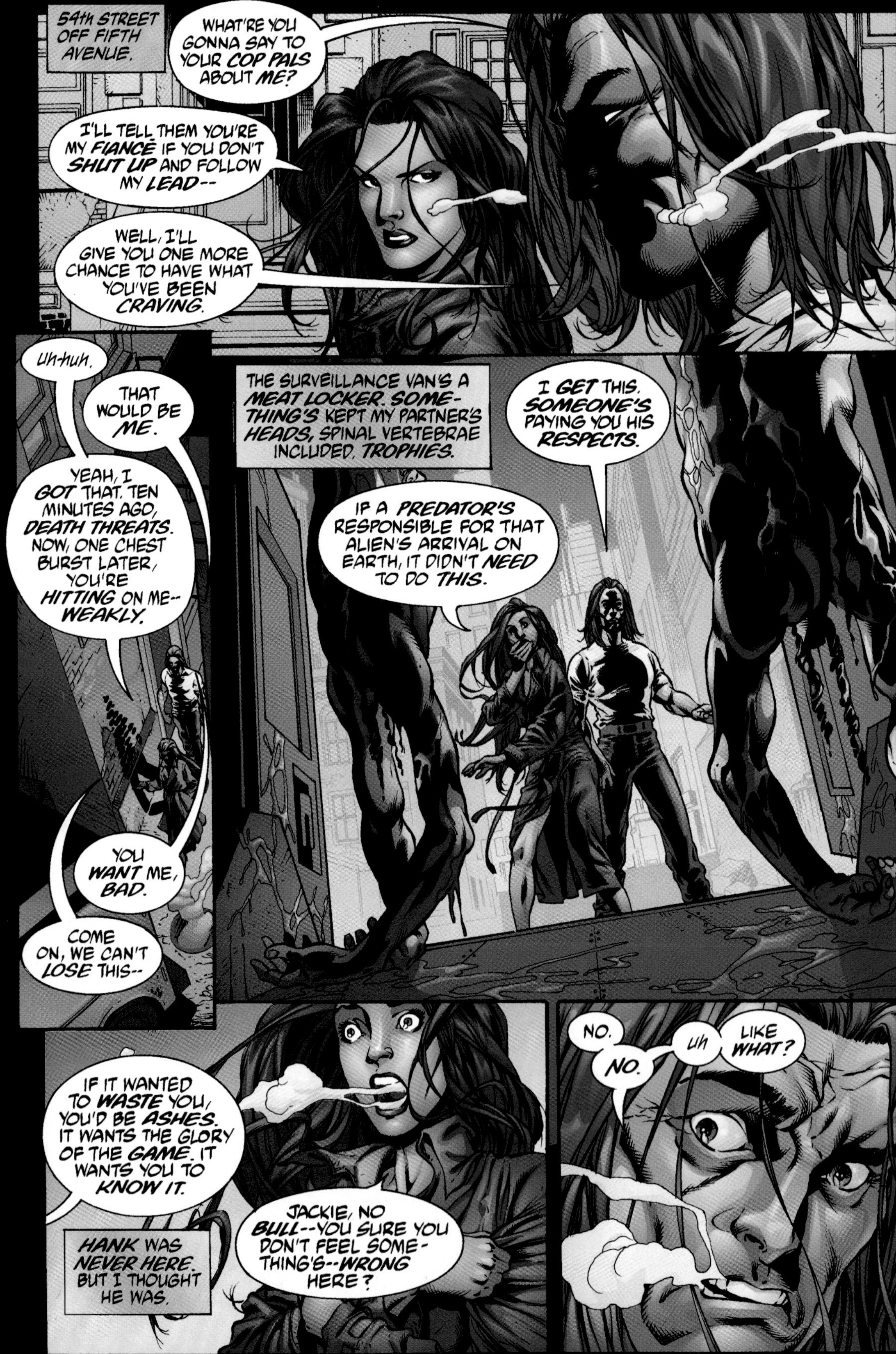
54th STREET OFF FIFTH AVENUE.
WHAT'RE YOU GONNA SAY TO YOUR COP PALS ABOUT ME?
I'LL TELL THEM YOU'RE MY FIANCÉ IF YOU DON'T SHUT UP AND FOLLOW MY LEAD--
WELL, I'LL GIVE YOU ONE MORE CHANCE TO HAVE WHAT YOU'VE BEEN CRAVING.
uh-huh.
THAT WOULD BE ME.
YEAH, I GOT THAT. TEN MINUTES AGO, DEATH THREATS. NOW, ONE CHEST BURST LATER, YOU'RE HITTING ON ME--WEAKLY.
YOU WANT ME, BAD.
COME ON, WE CAN'T LOSE THIS--
THE SURVEILLANCE VAN'S A MEAT LOCKER. SOMETHING'S KEPT MY PARTNER'S HEADS, SPINAL VERTEBRAE INCLUDED. TROPHIES.
I GET THIS. SOMEONE'S PAYING YOU HIS RESPECTS.
IF A PREDATOR'S RESPONSIBLE FOR THAT ALIEN'S ARRIVAL ON EARTH, IT DIDN'T NEED TO DO THIS.
IF IT WANTED TO WASTE YOU, YOU'D BE ASHES. IT WANTS THE GLORY OF THE GAME. IT WANTS YOU TO KNOW IT.
HANK WAS NEVER HERE. BUT I THOUGHT HE WAS.
JACKIE, NO BULL--YOU SURE YOU DON'T FEEL SOMETHING'S--WRONG HERE?
NO.
NO.
uh
LIKE WHAT?

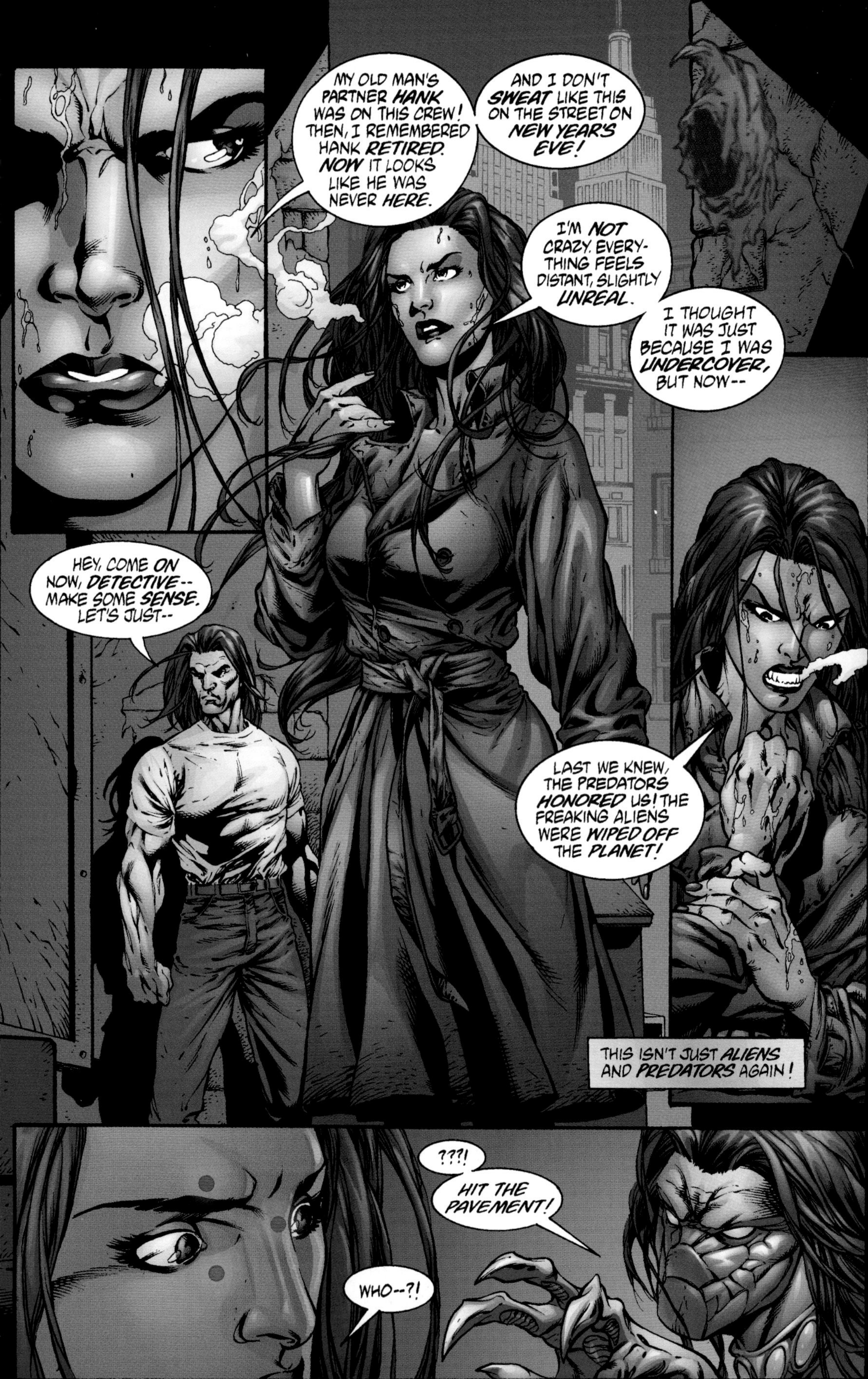
MY OLD MAN'S PARTNER HANK WAS ON THIS CREW! THEN, I REMEMBERED HANK RETIRED. NOW IT LOOKS LIKE HE WAS NEVER HERE.
AND I DON'T SWEAT LIKE THIS ON THE STREET ON NEW YEAR'S EVE!
I'M NOT CRAZY. EVERY-THING FEELS DISTANT, SLIGHTLY UNREAL.
I THOUGHT IT WAS JUST BECAUSE I WAS UNDERCOVER, BUT NOW--
HEY, COME ON NOW, DETECTIVE-- MAKE SOME SENSE. LET'S JUST--
LAST WE KNEW, THE PREDATORS HONORED US! THE FREAKING ALIENS WERE WIPED OFF THE PLANET!
THIS ISN'T JUST ALIENS AND PREDATORS AGAIN!
???!
HIT THE PAVEMENT!
WHO--?!

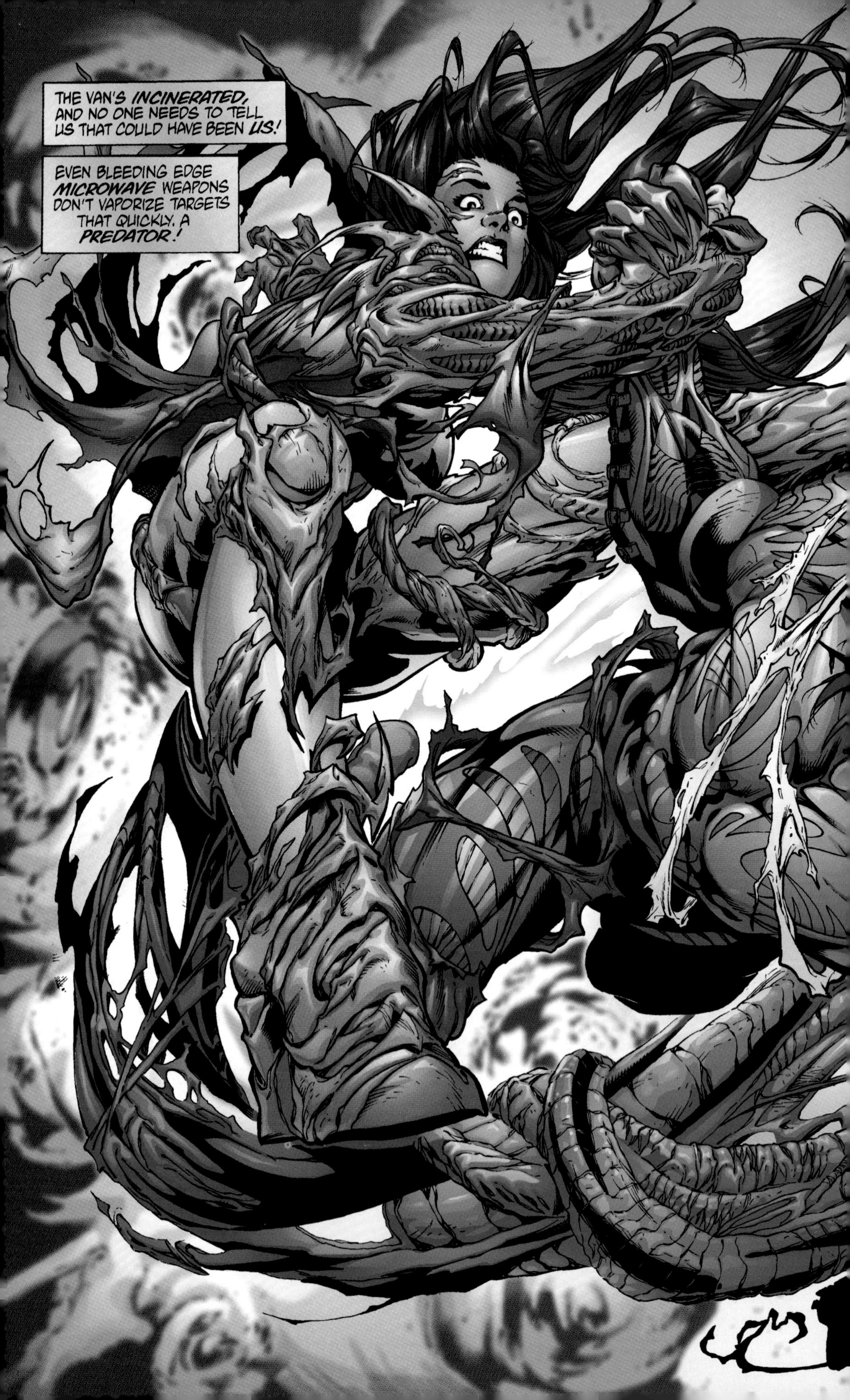
THE VAN'S INCINERATED, AND NO ONE NEEDS TO TELL US THAT COULD HAVE BEEN US!
EVEN BLEEDING EDGE MICROWAVE WEAPONS DON'T VAPORIZE TARGETS THAT QUICKLY. A PREDATOR!

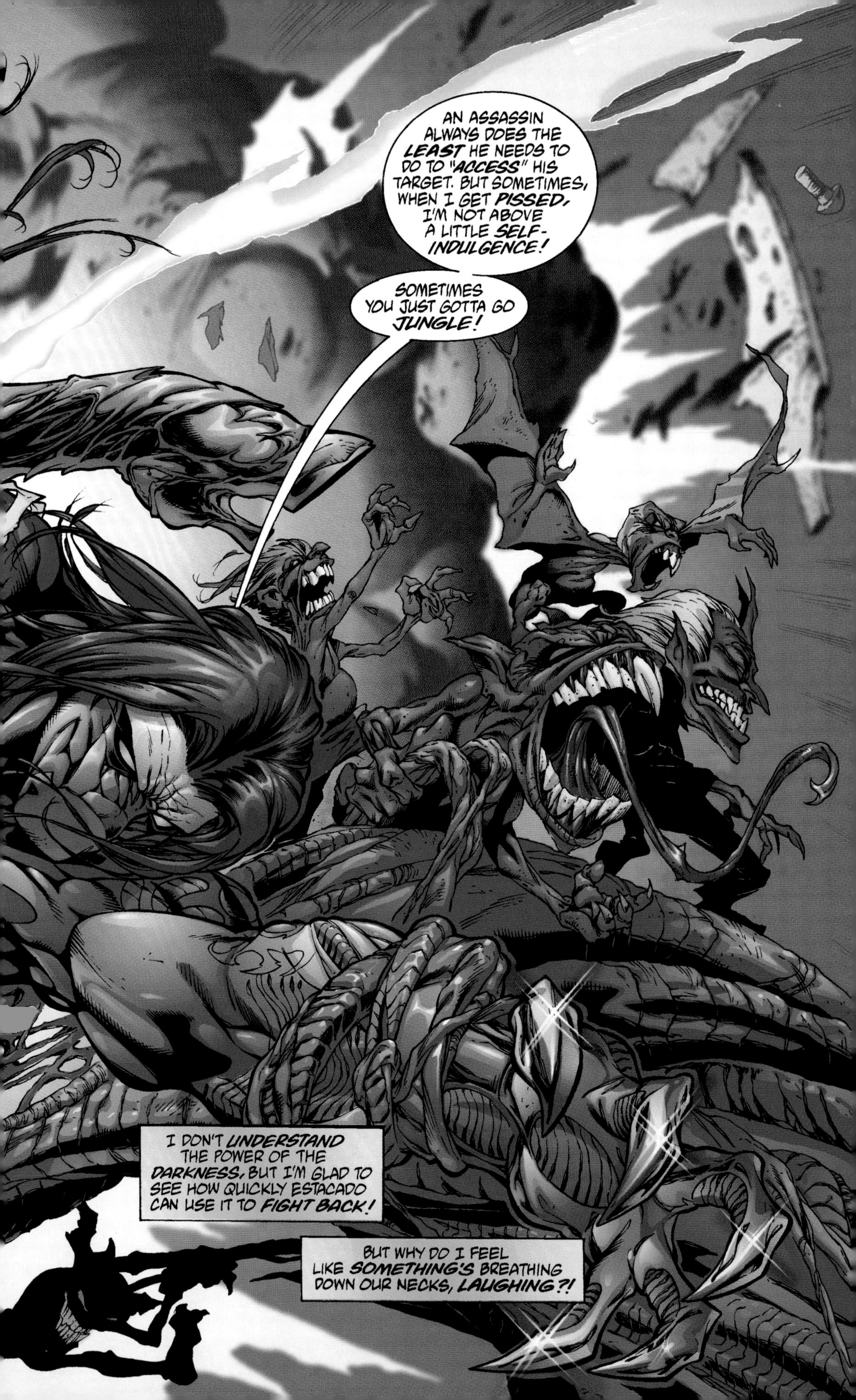
AN ASSASSIN ALWAYS DOES THE LEAST HE NEEDS TO DO TO "ACCESS" HIS TARGET. BUT SOMETIMES, WHEN I GET PISSED, I'M NOT ABOVE A LITTLE SELF-INDULGENCE!
SOMETIMES YOU JUST GOTTA GO JUNGLE!
I DON'T UNDERSTAND THE POWER OF THE DARKNESS, BUT I'M GLAD TO SEE HOW QUICKLY ESTACADO CAN USE IT TO FIGHT BACK!
BUT WHY DO I FEEL LIKE SOMETHING'S BREATHING DOWN OUR NECKS, LAUGHING?!

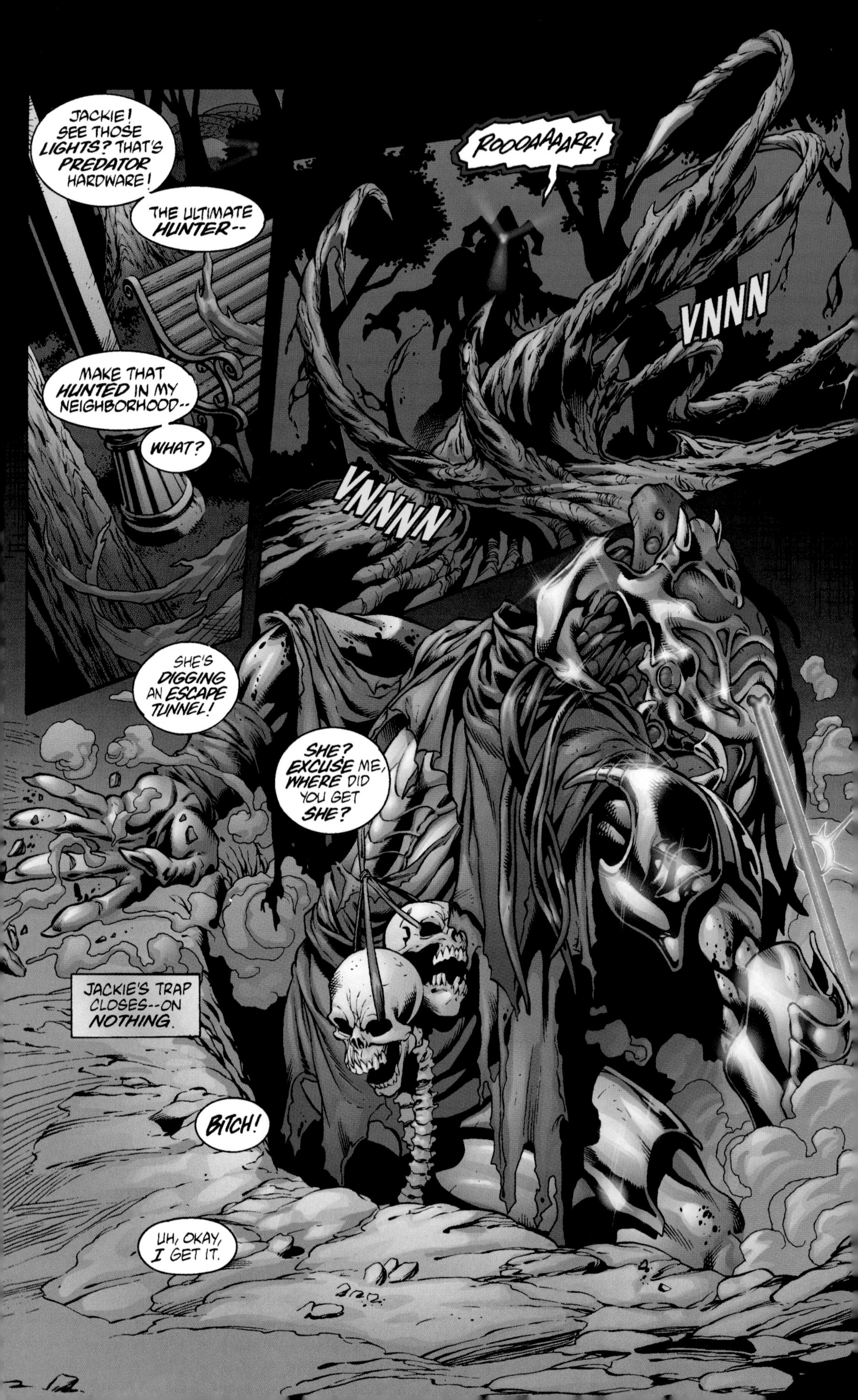
JACKIE! SEE THOSE LIGHTS? THAT'S PREDATOR HARDWARE!
THE ULTIMATE HUNTER--
ROOOAAAARR!
VNNN
MAKE THAT HUNTED IN MY NEIGHBORHOOD--
WHAT?
VNNNN
SHE'S DIGGING AN ESCAPE TUNNEL!
SHE? EXCUSE ME, WHERE DID YOU GET SHE?
JACKIE'S TRAP CLOSES--ON NOTHING.
BITCH!
UH, OKAY, I GET IT.

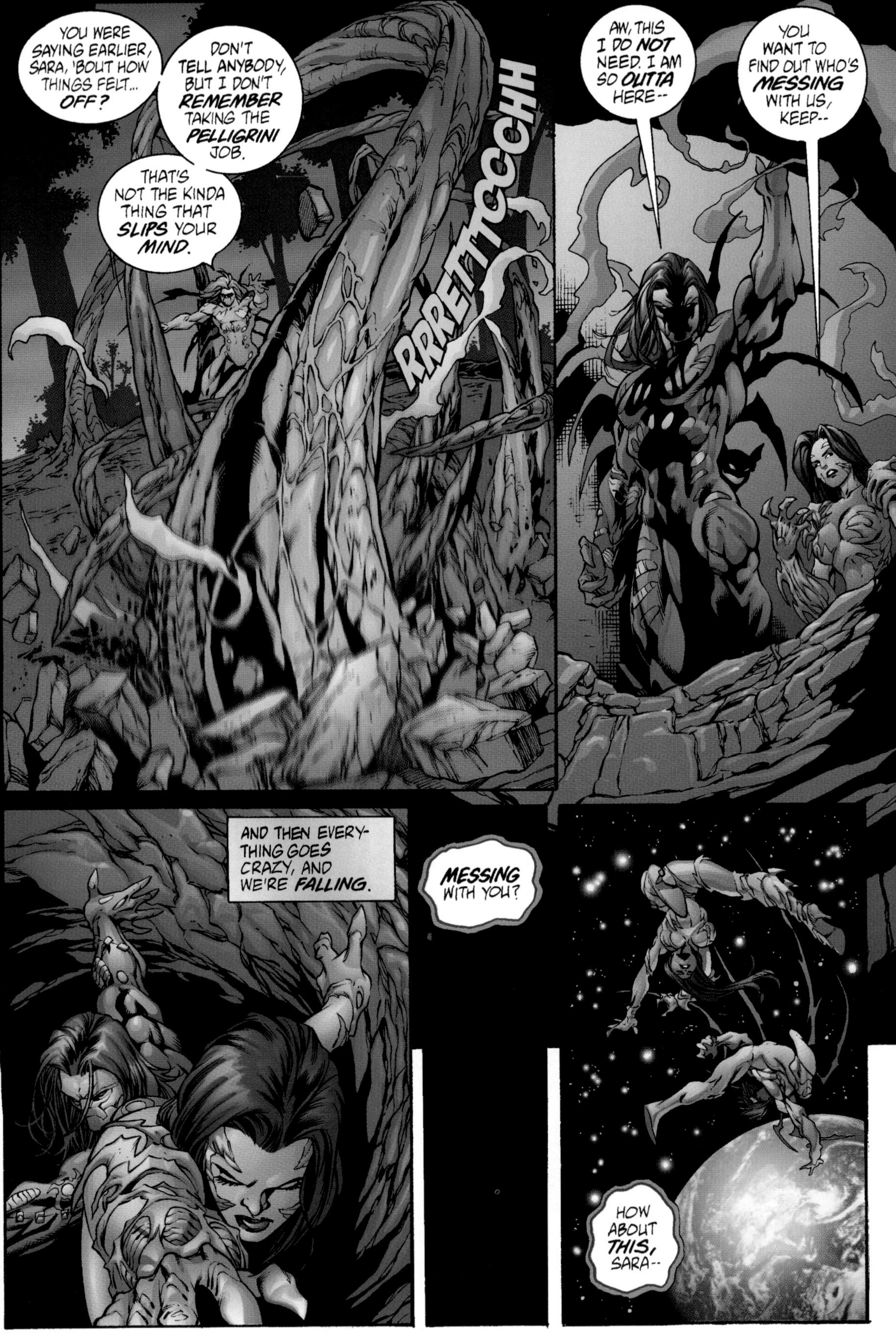

YOU WERE SAYING EARLIER, SARA, 'BOUT HOW THINGS FELT... OFF?
DON'T TELL ANYBODY, BUT I DON'T REMEMBER TAKING THE PELLIGRINI JOB.
THAT'S NOT THE KINDA THING THAT SLIPS YOUR MIND.
RRRETTCCHH
AW, THIS I DO NOT NEED. I AM SO OUTTA HERE--
YOU WANT TO FIND OUT WHO'S MESSING WITH US, KEEP--
AND THEN EVERYTHING GOES CRAZY, AND WE'RE FALLING.
MESSING WITH YOU?
HOW ABOUT THIS, SARA--

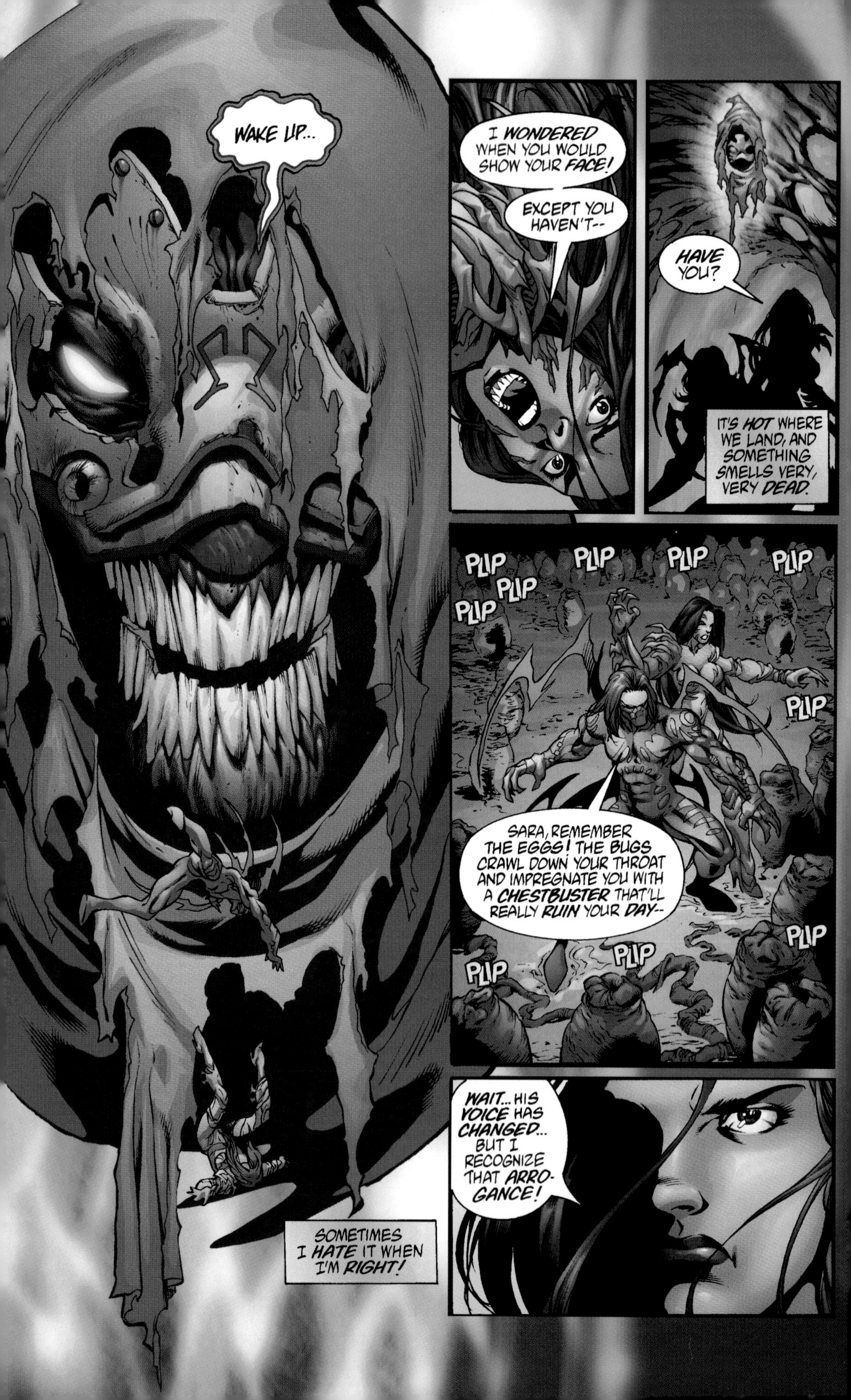
WAKE UP...
SOMETIMES I HATE IT WHEN I'M RIGHT!
I WONDERED WHEN YOU WOULD SHOW YOUR FACE!
EXCEPT YOU HAVEN'T--
HAVE YOU?
IT'S HOT WHERE WE LAND, AND SOMETHING SMELLS VERY, VERY DEAD.
PLIP PLIP PLIP PLIP PLIP PLIP
SARA, REMEMBER THE EGGS! THE BUGS CRAWL DOWN YOUR THROAT AND IMPREGNATE YOU WITH A CHESTBUSTER THAT'LL REALLY RUIN YOUR DAY--
PLIP PLIP PLIP PLIP
WAIT... HIS VOICE HAS CHANGED... BUT I RECOGNIZE THAT ARROGANCE!

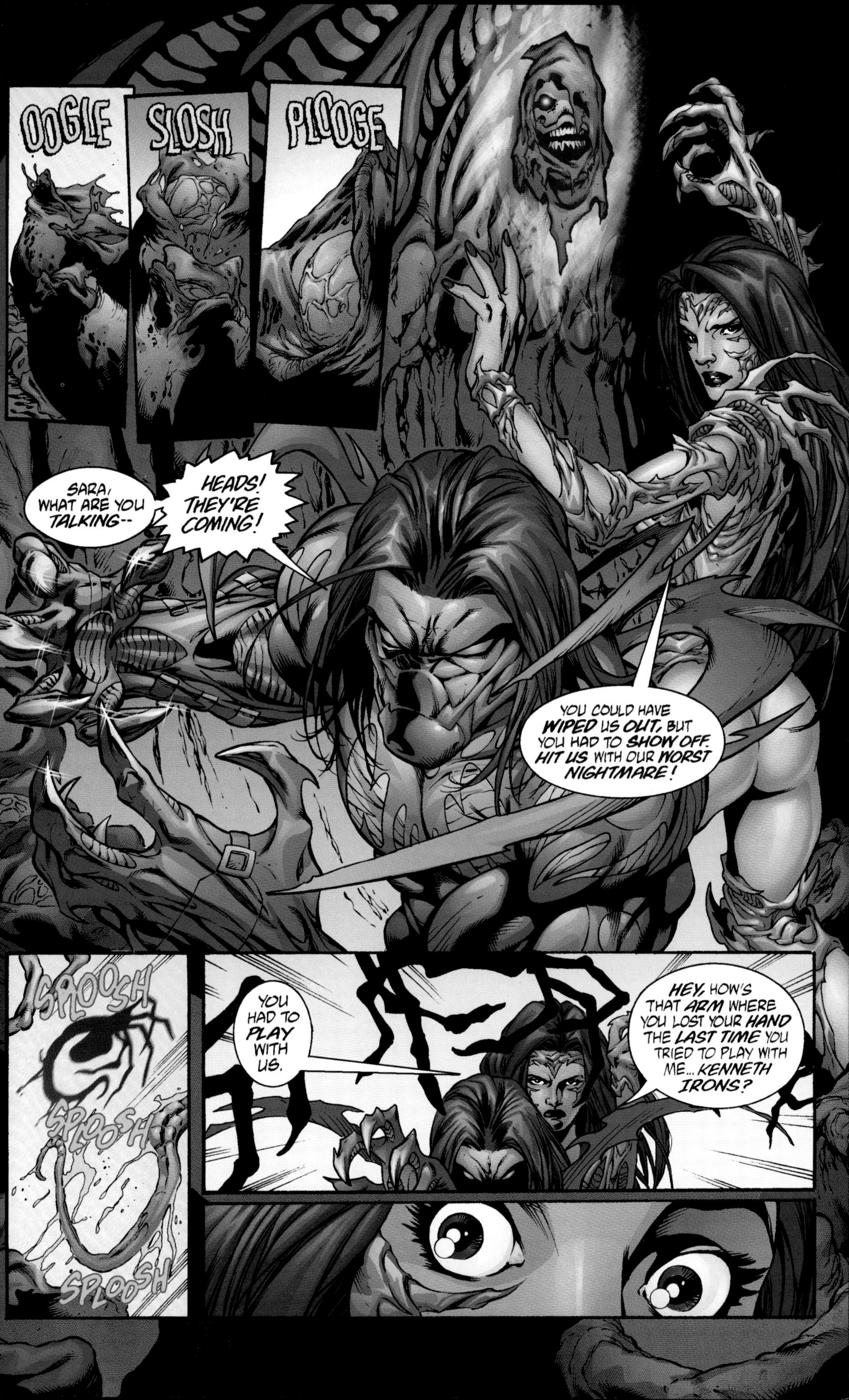
OOGLE
SLOSH
PLOOGE
SARA, WHAT ARE YOU TALKING--
HEADS! THEY'RE COMING!
YOU COULD HAVE WIPED US OUT, BUT YOU HAD TO SHOW OFF. HIT US WITH OUR WORST NIGHTMARE!
SPLOOSH
SPLOOSH
SPLOOSH
YOU HAD TO PLAY WITH US.
HEY, HOW'S THAT ARM WHERE YOU LOST YOUR HAND THE LAST TIME YOU TRIED TO PLAY WITH ME... KENNETH IRONS?

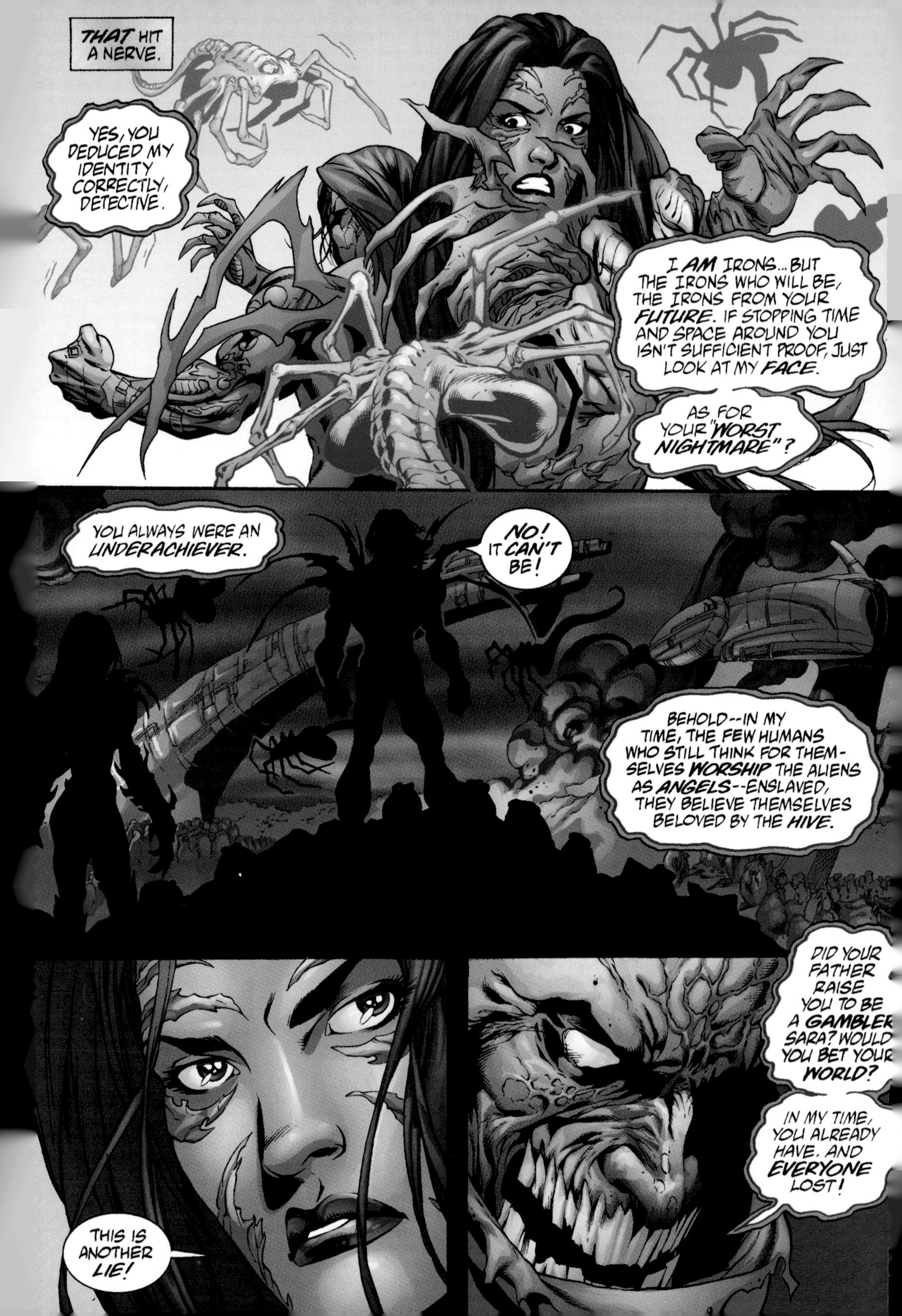
THAT HIT A NERVE.
YES, YOU DEDUCED MY IDENTITY CORRECTLY, DETECTIVE.
I AM IRONS... BUT THE IRONS WHO WILL BE, THE IRONS FROM YOUR FUTURE. IF STOPPING TIME AND SPACE AROUND YOU ISN'T SUFFICIENT PROOF, JUST LOOK AT MY FACE.
AS FOR YOUR "WORST NIGHTMARE"?
YOU ALWAYS WERE AN UNDERACHIEVER.
NO! IT CAN'T BE!
BEHOLD--IN MY TIME, THE FEW HUMANS WHO STILL THINK FOR THEM-SELVES WORSHIP THE ALIENS AS ANGELS--ENSLAVED, THEY BELIEVE THEMSELVES BELOVED BY THE HIVE.
DID YOUR FATHER RAISE YOU TO BE A GAMBLER, SARA? WOULD YOU BET YOUR WORLD?
IN MY TIME, YOU ALREADY HAVE. AND EVERYONE LOST!
THIS IS ANOTHER LIE!

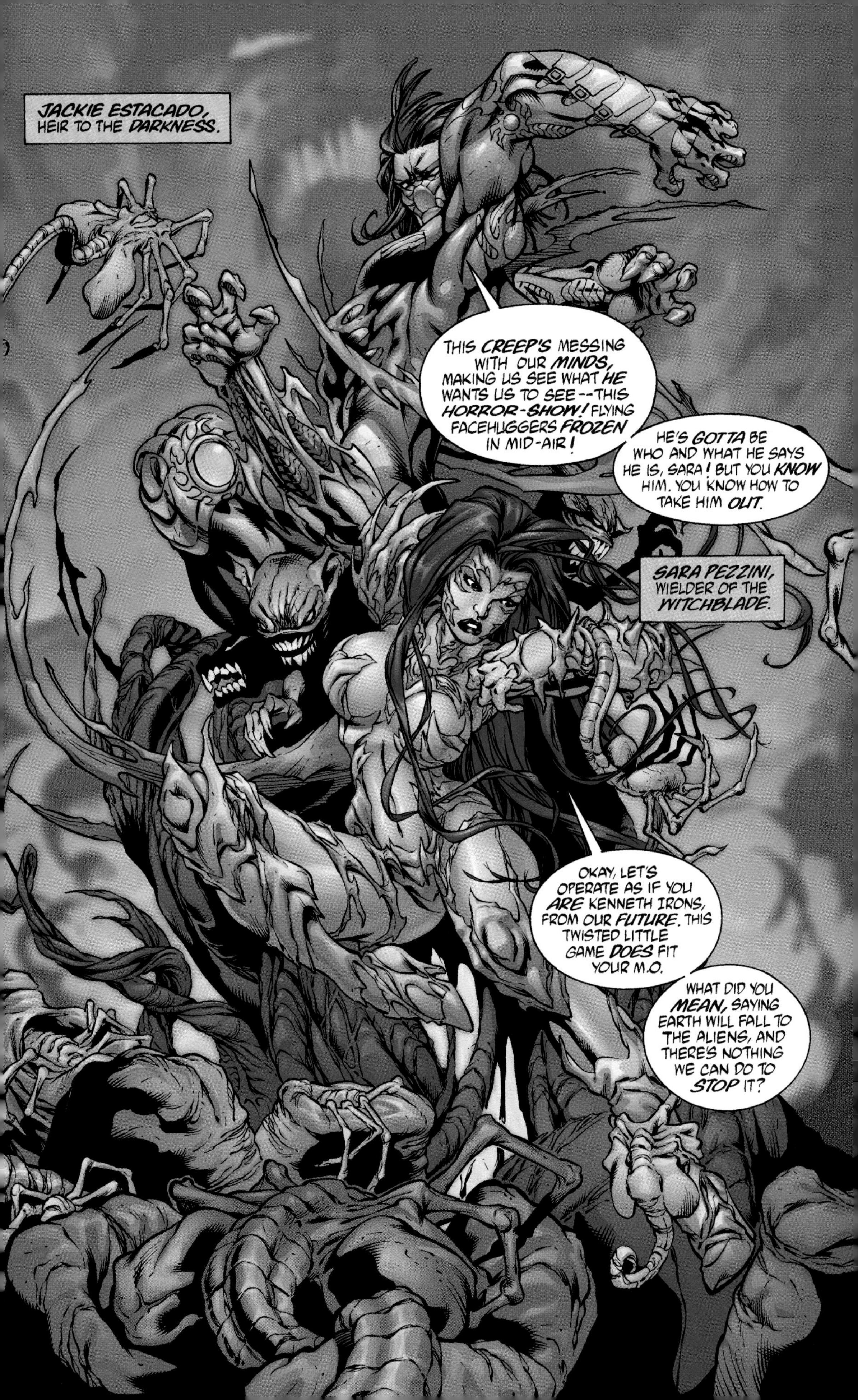
JACKIE ESTACADO, HEIR TO THE DARKNESS.
THIS CREEP'S MESSING WITH OUR MINDS, MAKING US SEE WHAT HE WANTS US TO SEE--THIS HORROR-SHOW! FLYING FACEHUGGERS FROZEN IN MID-AIR!
HE'S GOTTA BE WHO AND WHAT HE SAYS HE IS, SARA! BUT YOU KNOW HIM. YOU KNOW HOW TO TAKE HIM OUT.
SARA PEZZINI, WIELDER OF THE WITCHBLADE.
OKAY, LET'S OPERATE AS IF YOU ARE KENNETH IRONS, FROM OUR FUTURE. THIS TWISTED LITTLE GAME DOES FIT YOUR M.O.
WHAT DID YOU MEAN, SAYING EARTH WILL FALL TO THE ALIENS, AND THERE'S NOTHING WE CAN DO TO STOP IT?

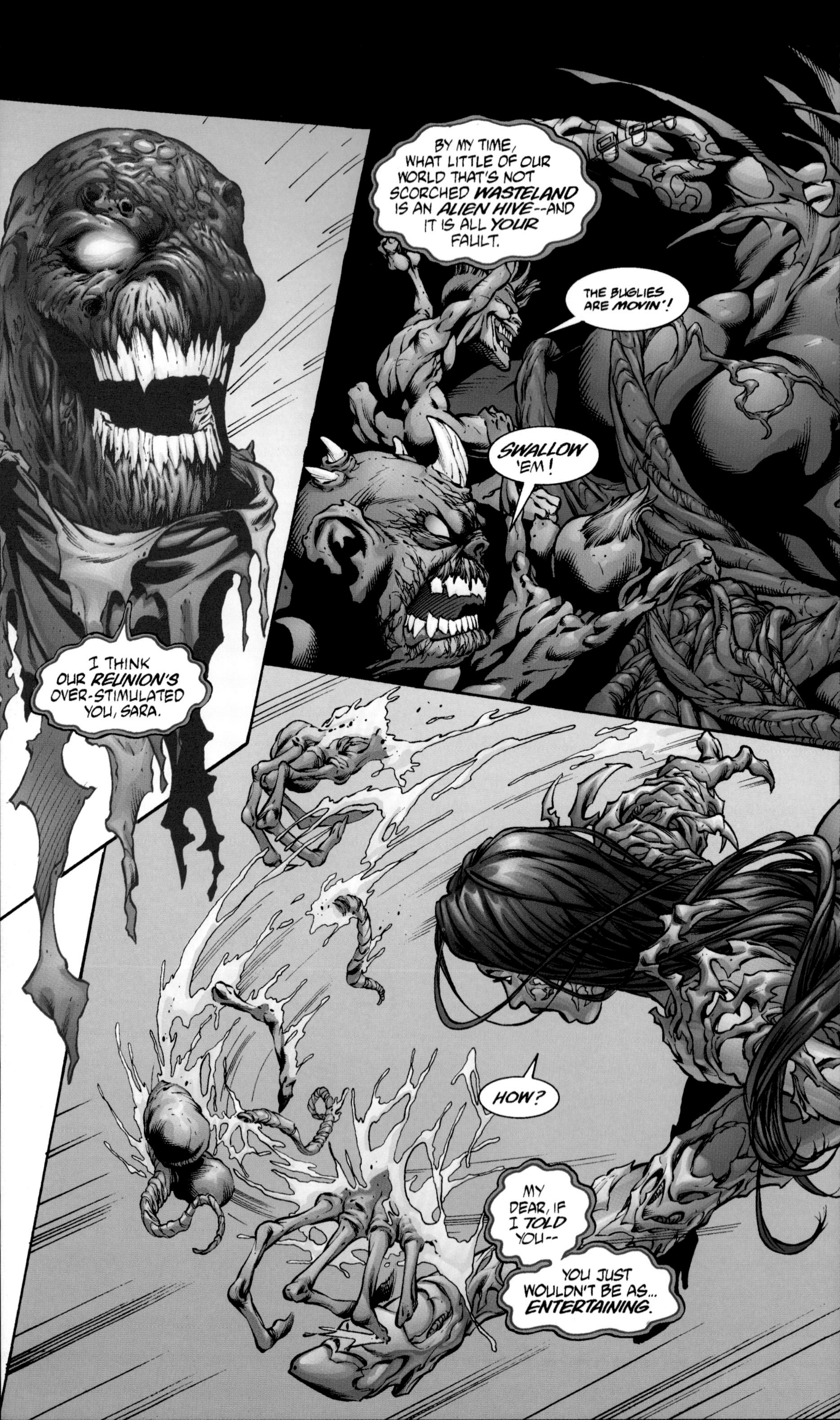
BY MY TIME, WHAT LITTLE OF OUR WORLD THAT'S NOT SCORCHED WASTELAND IS AN ALIEN HIVE--AND IT IS ALL YOUR FAULT.
THE BUGLIES ARE MOVIN'!
SWALLOW 'EM!
I THINK OUR REUNION'S OVER-STIMULATED YOU, SARA.
HOW?
MY DEAR, IF I TOLD YOU--
YOU JUST WOULDN'T BE AS... ENTERTAINING.

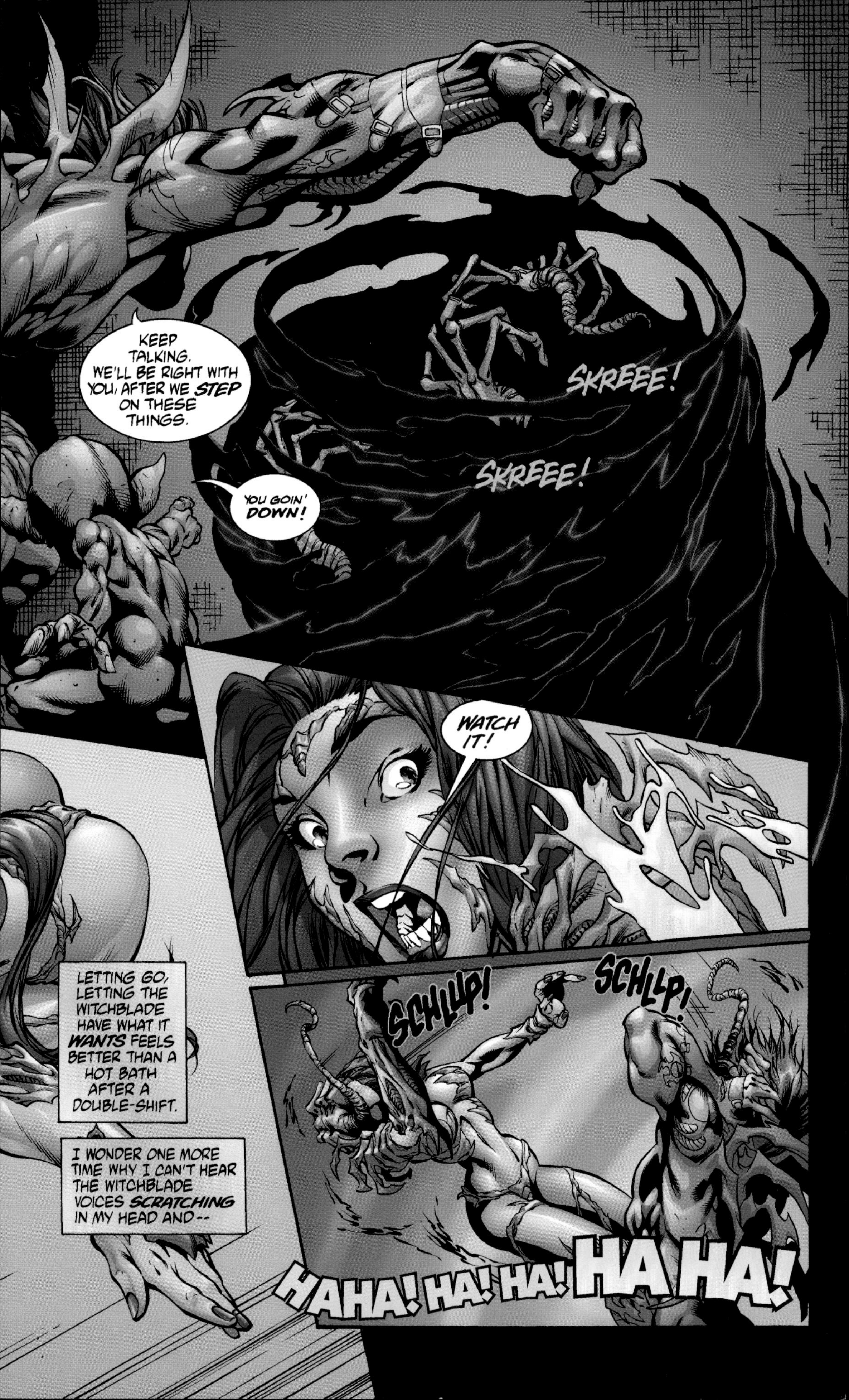
KEEP TALKING. WE'LL BE RIGHT WITH YOU, AFTER WE STEP ON THESE THINGS.
SKREEE!
SKREEE!
YOU GOIN' DOWN!
WATCH IT!
LETTING GO, LETTING THE WITCHBLADE HAVE WHAT IT WANTS FEELS BETTER THAN A HOT BATH AFTER A DOUBLE-SHIFT.
I WONDER ONE MORE TIME WHY I CAN'T HEAR THE WITCHBLADE VOICES SCRATCHING IN MY HEAD AND--
SCHLUP!
SCHLLP!
HAHA! HA! HA! HA HA!

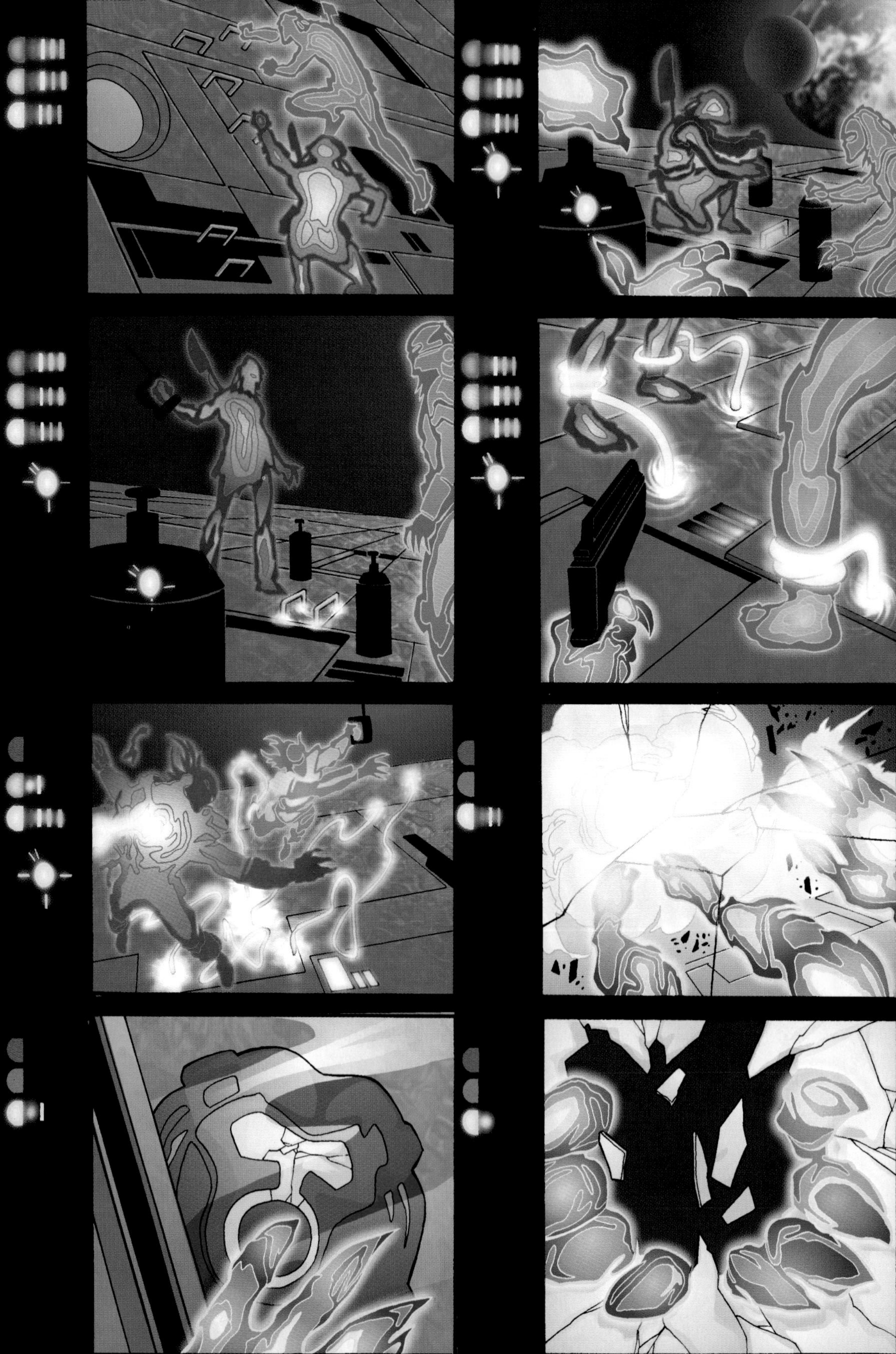

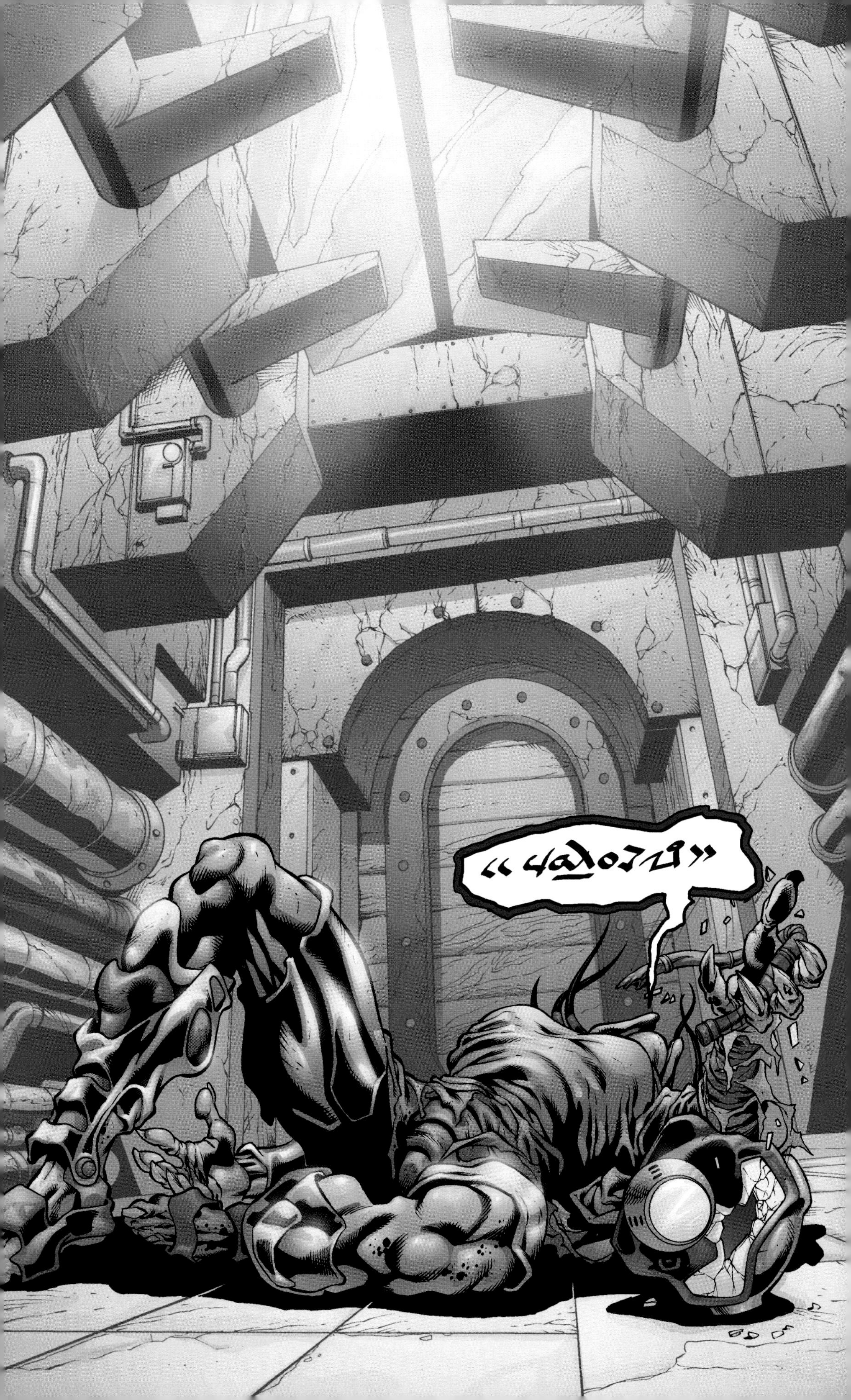

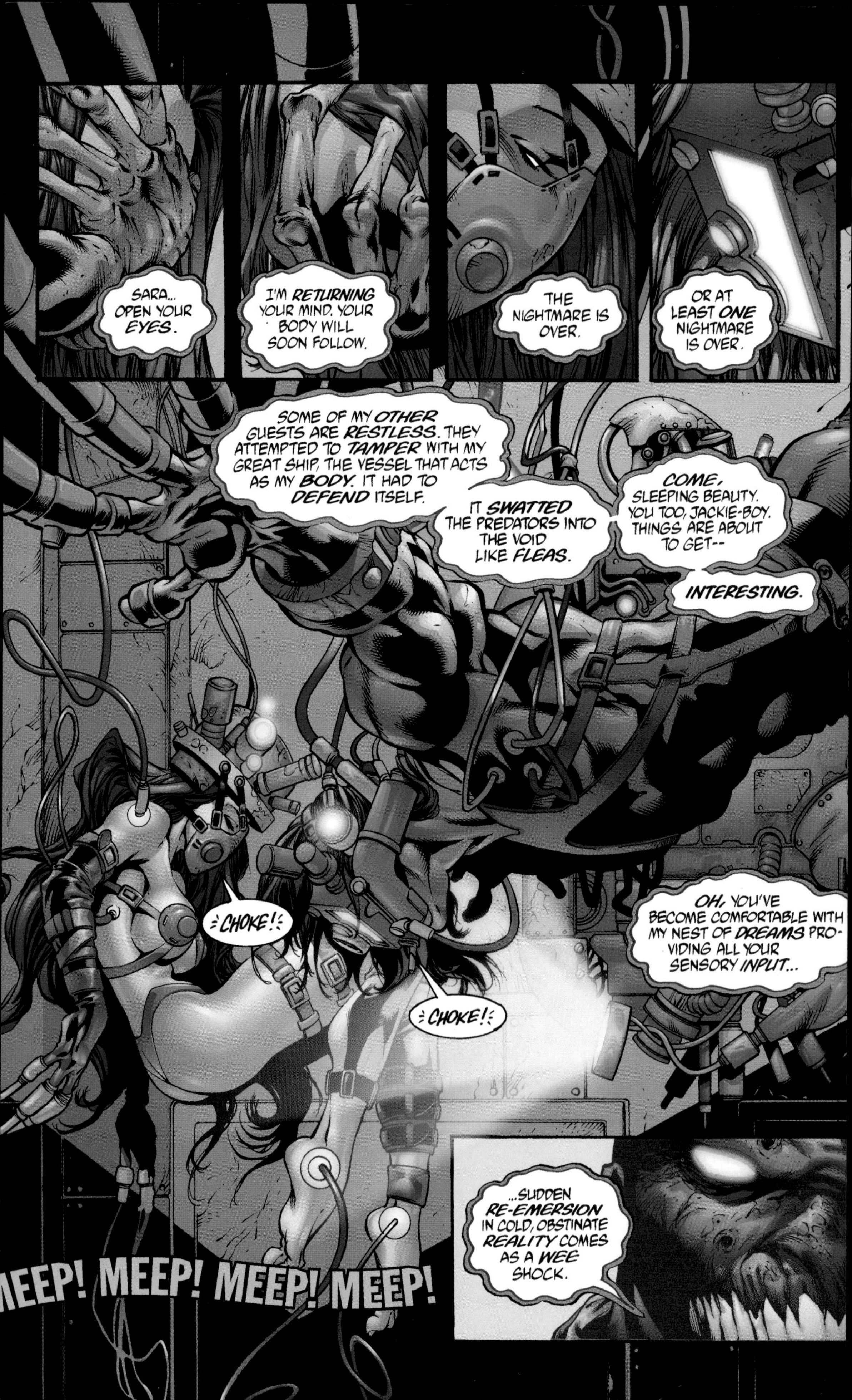
SARA... OPEN YOUR EYES.
I'M RETURNING YOUR MIND. YOUR BODY WILL SOON FOLLOW.
THE NIGHTMARE IS OVER.
OR AT LEAST ONE NIGHTMARE IS OVER.
SOME OF MY OTHER GUESTS ARE RESTLESS. THEY ATTEMPTED TO TAMPER WITH MY GREAT SHIP, THE VESSEL THAT ACTS AS MY BODY. IT HAD TO DEFEND ITSELF.
IT SWATTED THE PREDATORS INTO THE VOID LIKE FLEAS.
COME, SLEEPING BEAUTY. YOU TOO, JACKIE-BOY. THINGS ARE ABOUT TO GET--
INTERESTING.
CHOKE!
CHOKE!
OH, YOU'VE BECOME COMFORTABLE WITH MY NEST OF DREAMS PRO-VIDING ALL YOUR SENSORY INPUT...
MEEP! MEEP! MEEP! MEEP!
...SUDDEN RE-EMERSION IN COLD, OBSTINATE REALITY COMES AS A WEE SHOCK.

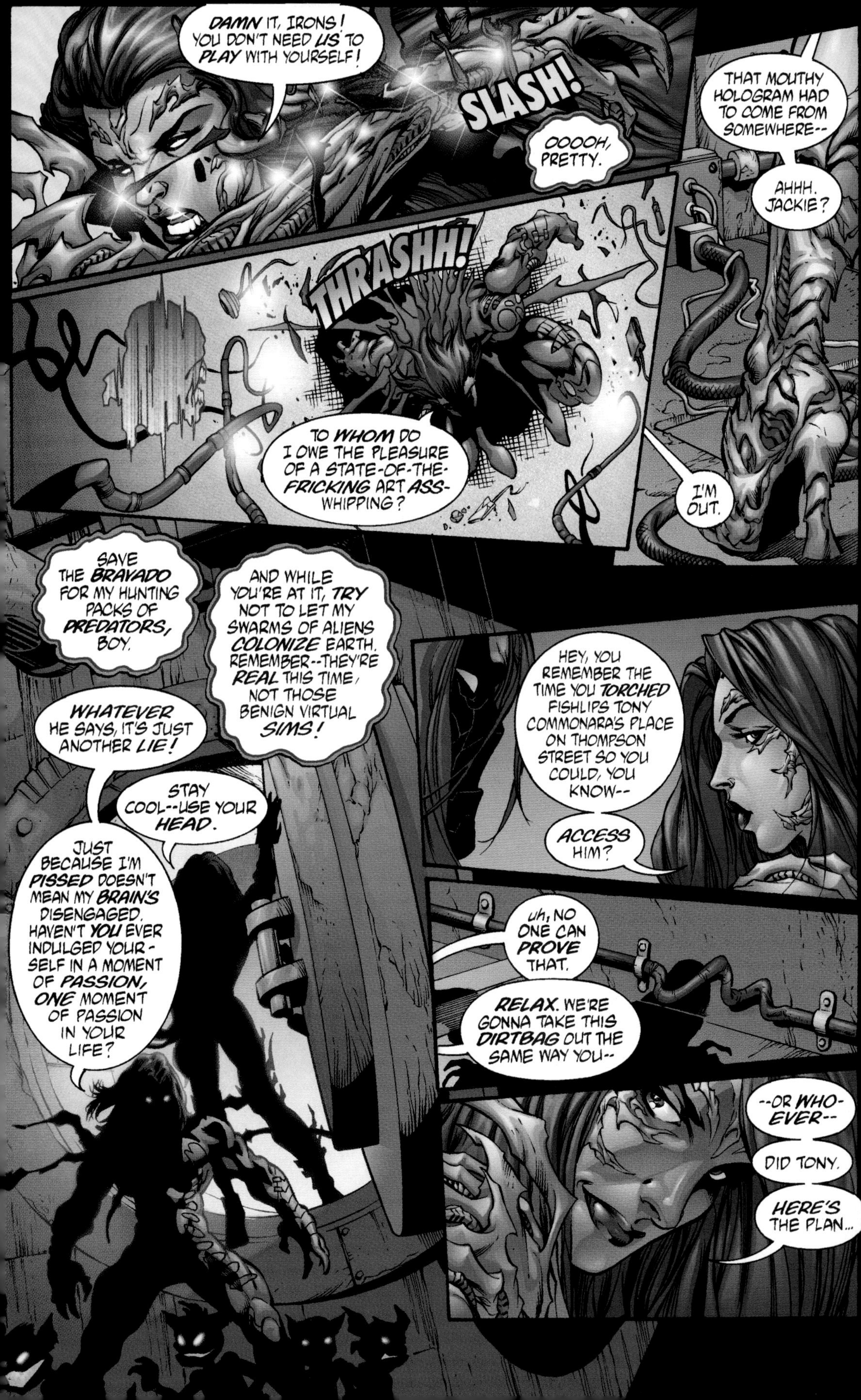
DAMN IT, IRONS! YOU DON'T NEED US TO PLAY WITH YOURSELF!
SLASH!
OOOOH, PRETTY.
THAT MOUTHY HOLOGRAM HAD TO COME FROM SOMEWHERE--
AHHH. JACKIE?
THRASHH!
TO WHOM DO I OWE THE PLEASURE OF A STATE-OF-THE-FRICKING ART ASS-WHIPPING?
I'M OUT.
SAVE THE BRAVADO FOR MY HUNTING PACKS OF PREDATORS, BOY.
AND WHILE YOU'RE AT IT, TRY NOT TO LET MY SWARMS OF ALIENS COLONIZE EARTH. REMEMBER--THEY'RE REAL THIS TIME, NOT THOSE BENIGN VIRTUAL SIMS!
WHATEVER HE SAYS, IT'S JUST ANOTHER LIE!
STAY COOL--USE YOUR HEAD.
JUST BECAUSE I'M PISSED DOESN'T MEAN MY BRAIN'S DISENGAGED. HAVEN'T YOU EVER INDULGED YOUR-SELF IN A MOMENT OF PASSION, ONE MOMENT OF PASSION IN YOUR LIFE?
HEY, YOU REMEMBER THE TIME YOU TORCHED FISHLIPS TONY COMMONARA'S PLACE ON THOMPSON STREET SO YOU COULD, YOU KNOW--
ACCESS HIM?
uh, NO ONE CAN PROVE THAT.
RELAX. WE'RE GONNA TAKE THIS DIRTBAG OUT THE SAME WAY YOU--
--OR WHO-EVER--
DID TONY.
HERE'S THE PLAN...

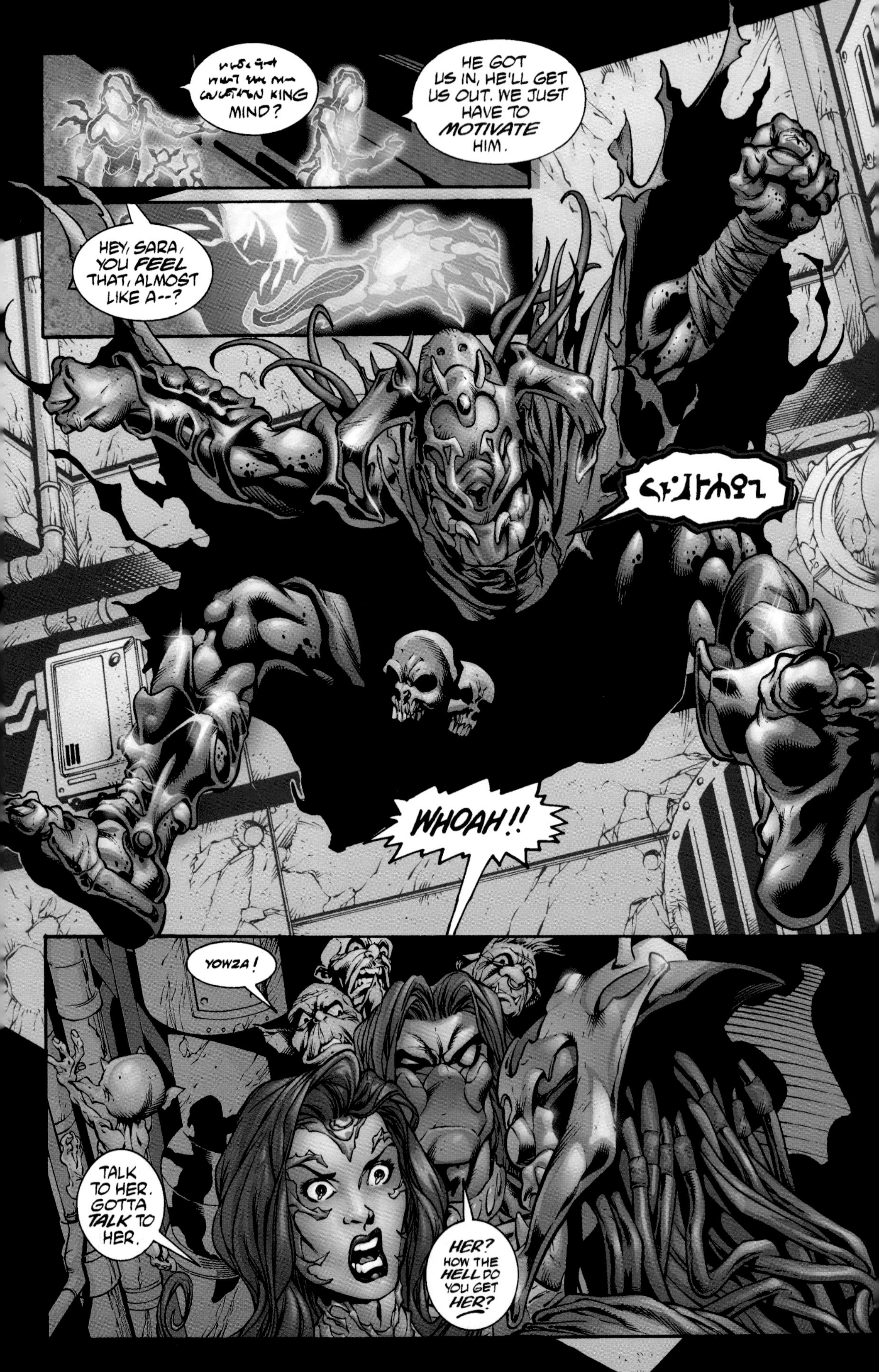

HE GOT US IN, HE'LL GET US OUT. WE JUST HAVE TO MOTIVATE HIM.
HEY, SARA, YOU FEEL THAT, ALMOST LIKE A--?
WHOAH!!
YOWZA!
TALK TO HER. GOTTA TALK TO HER.
HER? HOW THE HELL DO YOU GET HER?

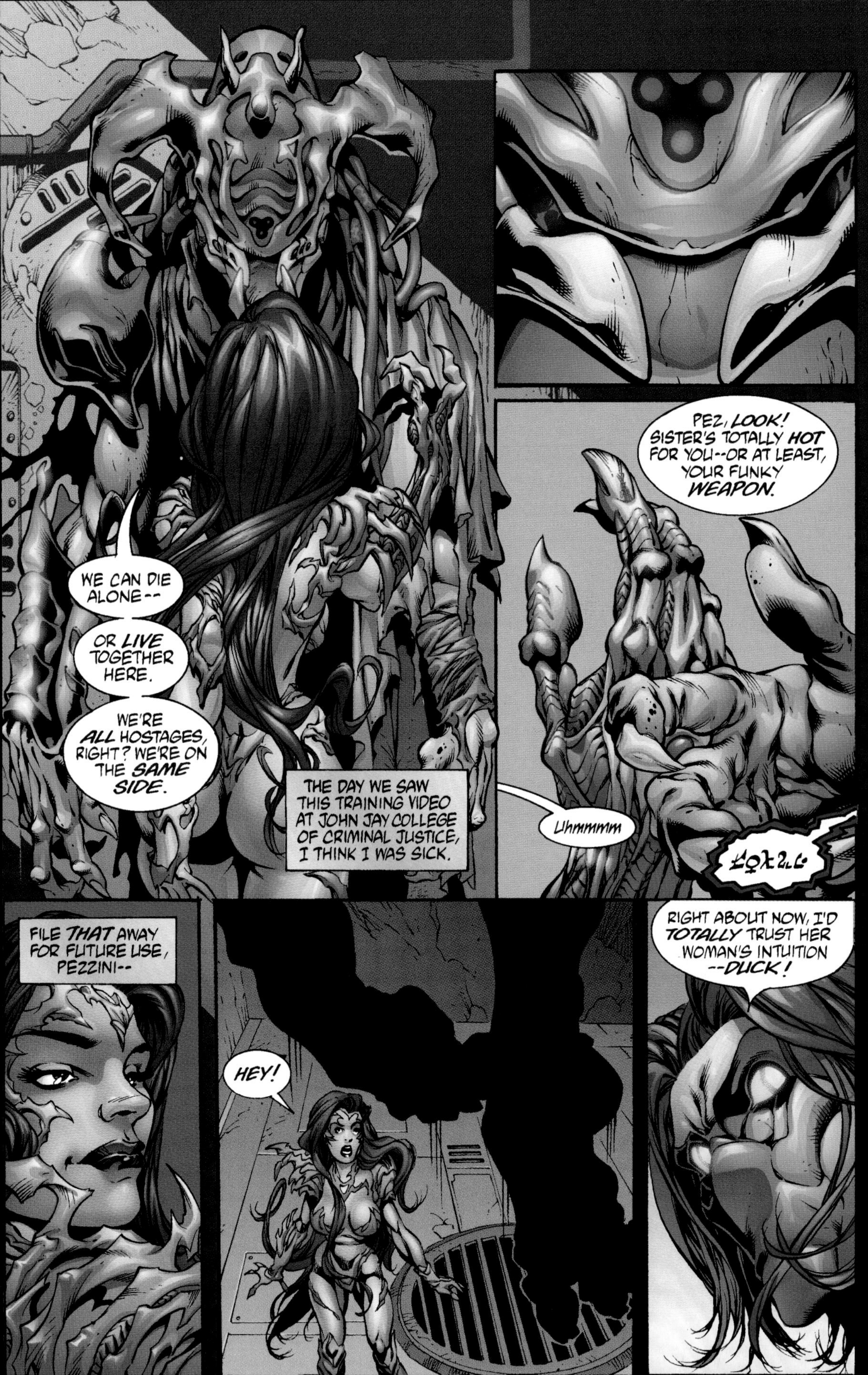
WE CAN DIE ALONE--
OR LIVE TOGETHER HERE.
WE'RE ALL HOSTAGES, RIGHT? WE'RE ON THE SAME SIDE.
THE DAY WE SAW THIS TRAINING VIDEO AT JOHN JAY COLLEGE OF CRIMINAL JUSTICE, I THINK I WAS SICK.
PEZ, LOOK! SISTER'S TOTALLY HOT FOR YOU--OR AT LEAST, YOUR FUNKY WEAPON.
Uhmmmm
FILE THAT AWAY FOR FUTURE USE, PEZZINI--
HEY!
RIGHT ABOUT NOW, I'D TOTALLY TRUST HER WOMAN'S INTUITION --DUCK!

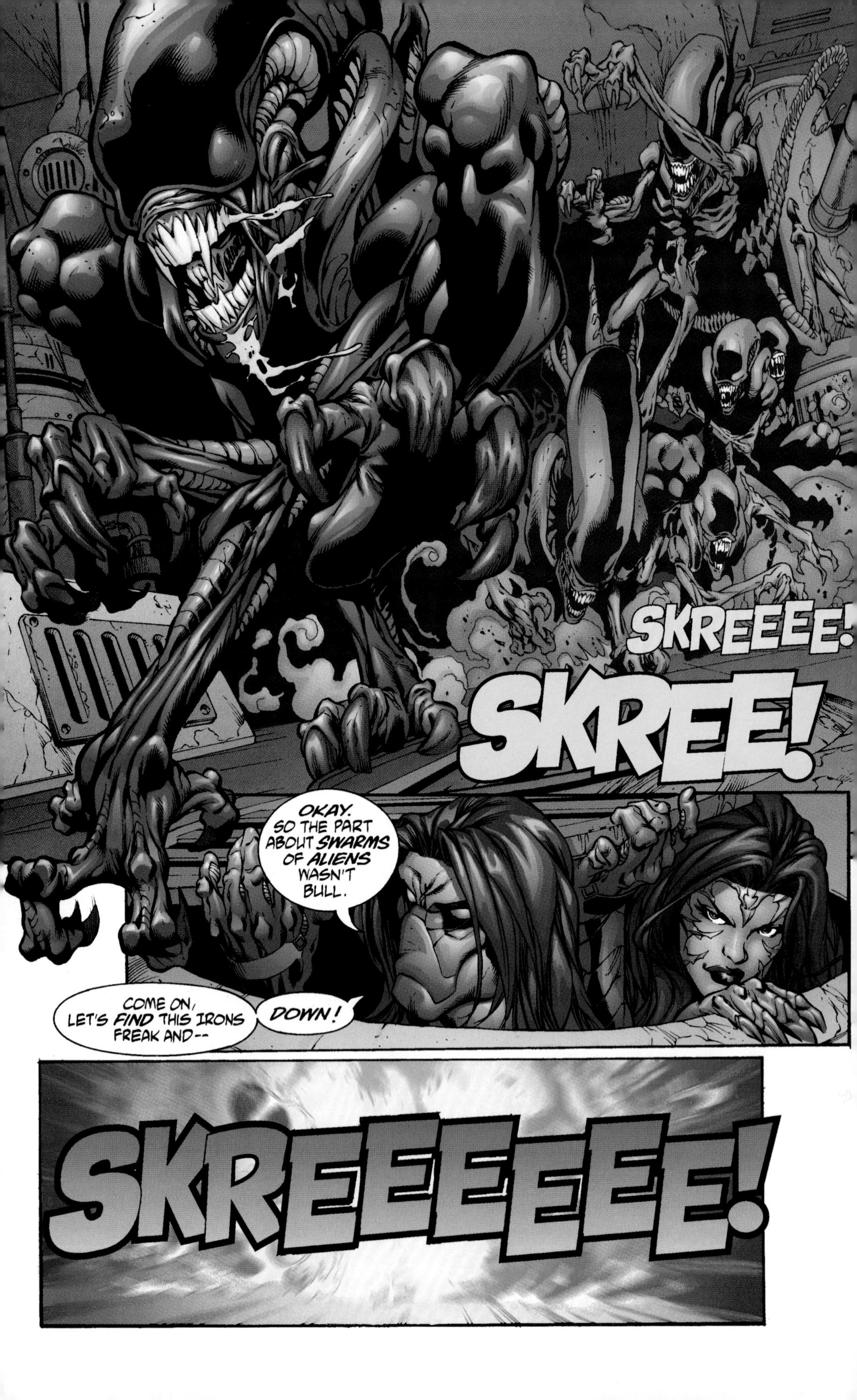
SKREEEEE!
SKREE!
OKAY. SO THE PART ABOUT SWARMS OF ALIENS WASN'T BULL.
COME ON, LET'S FIND THIS IRONS FREAK AND--
DOWN!
SKREEEEEEE!

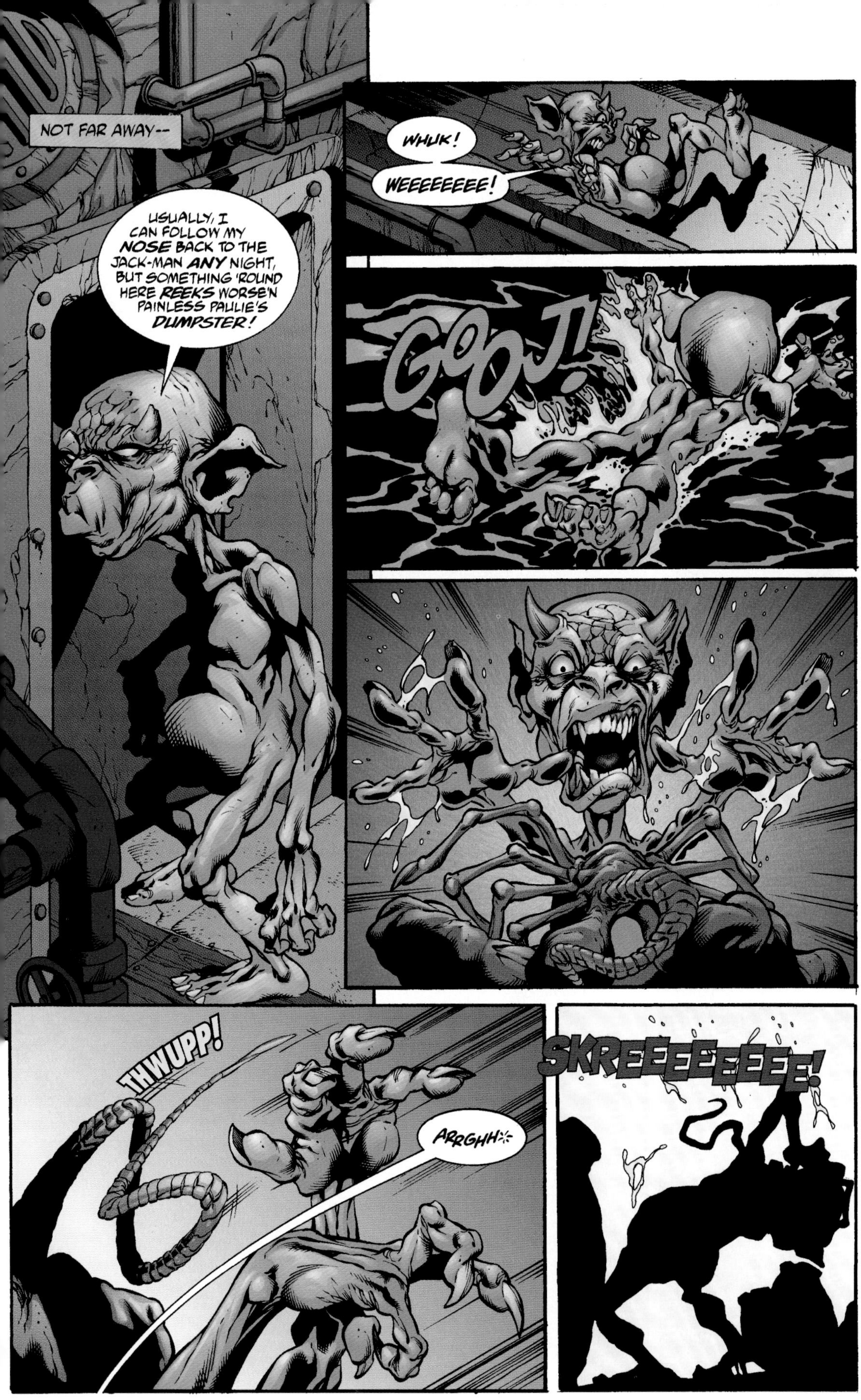
NOT FAR AWAY--
USUALLY, I CAN FOLLOW MY NOSE BACK TO THE JACK-MAN ANY NIGHT, BUT SOMETHING 'ROUND HERE REEKS WORSE'N PAINLESS PAULIE'S DUMPSTER!
WHUK!
WEEEEEEEE!
GOOJ!
THWUPP!
ARRGHH!
SKREEEEEEEEEE!

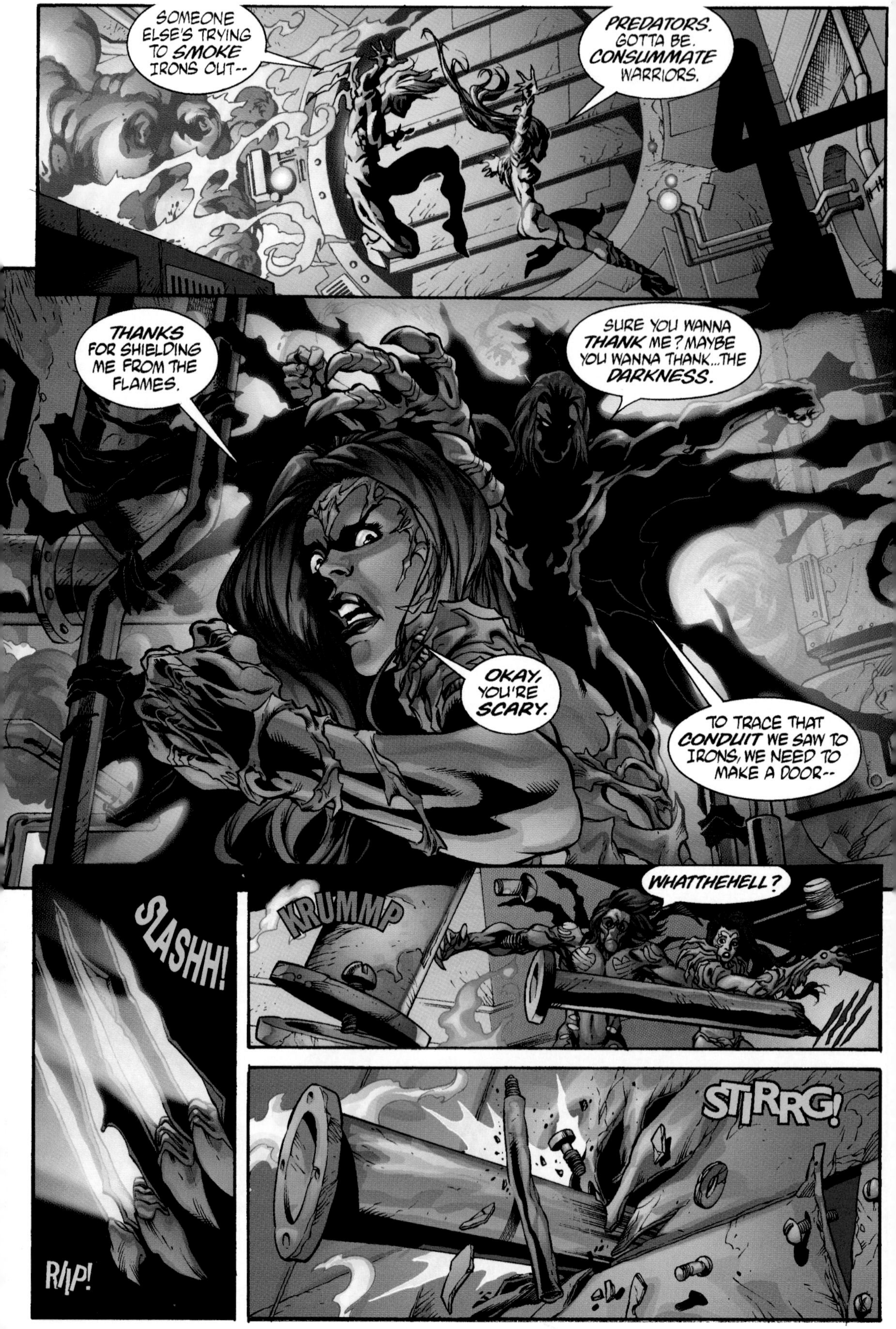
SOMEONE ELSE'S TRYING TO SMOKE IRONS OUT--
PREDATORS. GOTTA BE. CONSUMMATE WARRIORS.
THANKS FOR SHIELDING ME FROM THE FLAMES.
SURE YOU WANNA THANK ME? MAYBE YOU WANNA THANK...THE DARKNESS.
OKAY, YOU'RE SCARY.
TO TRACE THAT CONDUIT WE SAW TO IRONS, WE NEED TO MAKE A DOOR--
SLASHH!
RIP!
KRUMMP
WHATTHEHELL?
STIRRG!

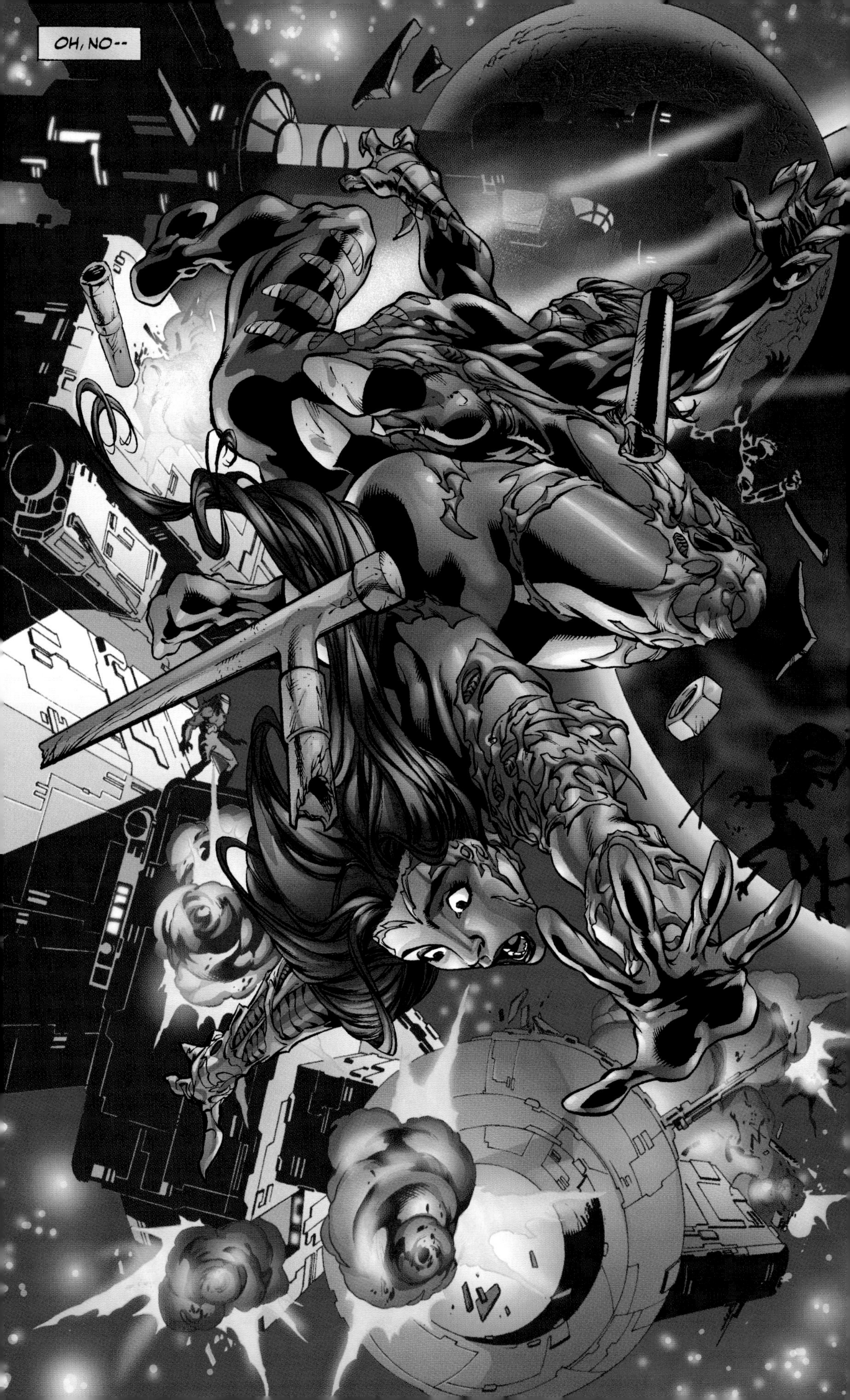
OH, NO--

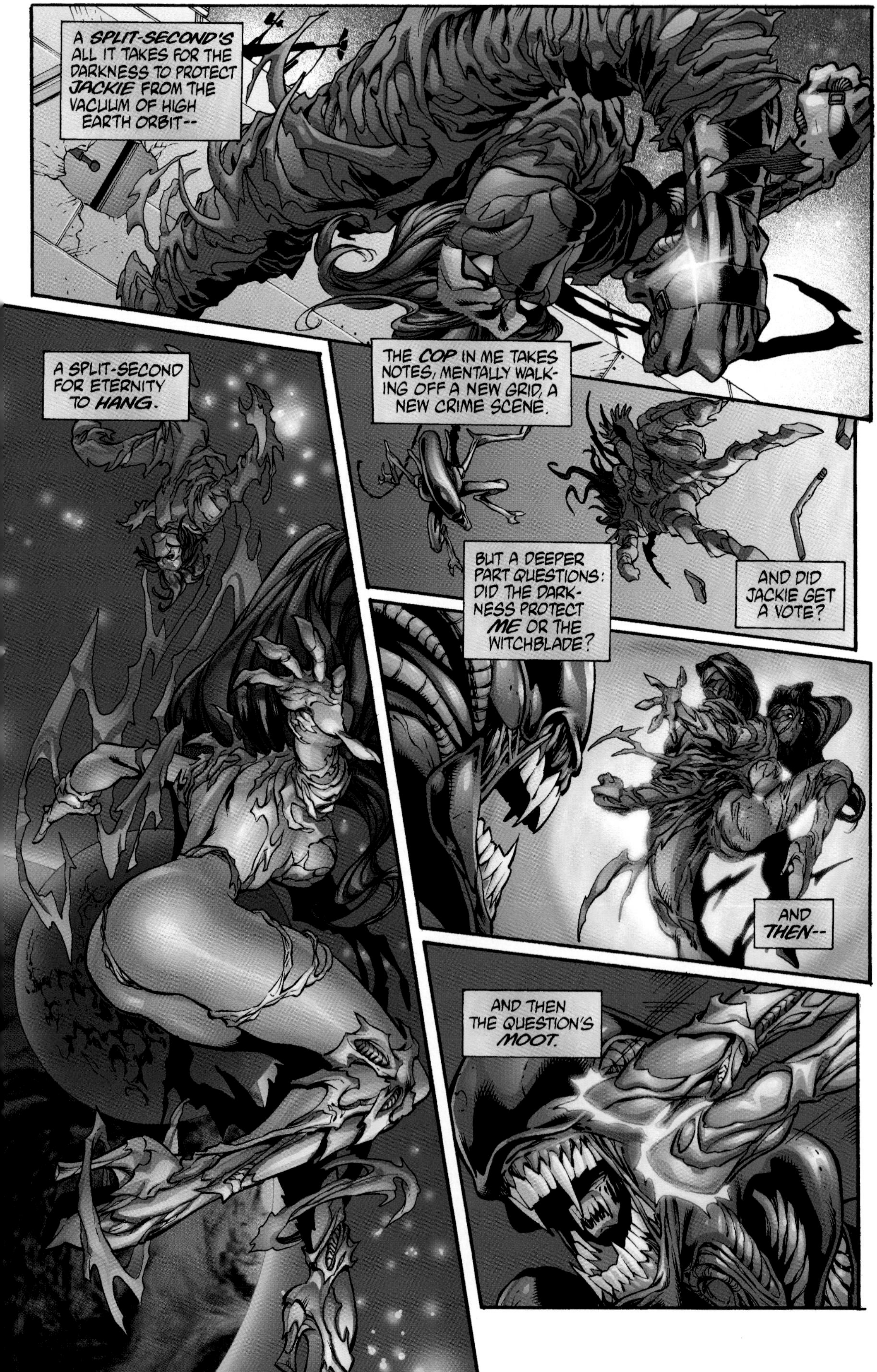
A SPLIT-SECOND'S ALL IT TAKES FOR THE DARKNESS TO PROTECT JACKIE FROM THE VACUUM OF HIGH EARTH ORBIT--
A SPLIT-SECOND FOR ETERNITY TO HANG.
THE COP IN ME TAKES NOTES, MENTALLY WALKING OFF A NEW GRID, A NEW CRIME SCENE.
BUT A DEEPER PART QUESTIONS: DID THE DARKNESS PROTECT ME OR THE WITCHBLADE?
AND DID JACKIE GET A VOTE?
AND THEN--
AND THEN THE QUESTION'S MOOT.

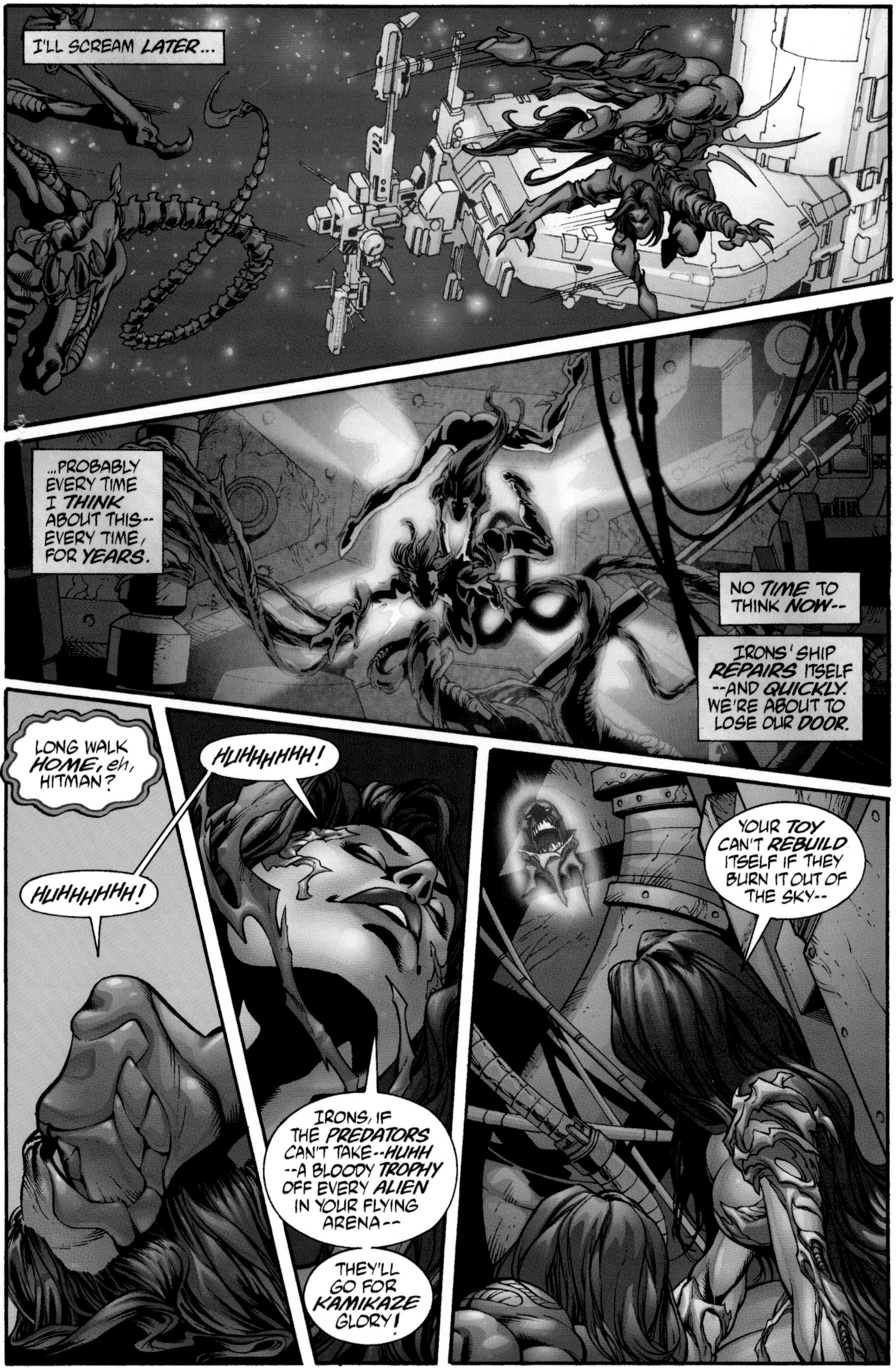

I'LL SCREAM LATER...
...PROBABLY EVERY TIME I THINK ABOUT THIS-- EVERY TIME, FOR YEARS.
NO TIME TO THINK NOW--
IRONS' SHIP REPAIRS ITSELF --AND QUICKLY. WE'RE ABOUT TO LOSE OUR DOOR.
LONG WALK HOME, eh, HITMAN?
HUHHHHHH!
HUHHHHHH!
IRONS, IF THE PREDATORS CAN'T TAKE--HUHH --A BLOODY TROPHY OFF EVERY ALIEN IN YOUR FLYING ARENA--
THEY'LL GO FOR KAMIKAZE GLORY!
YOUR TOY CAN'T REBUILD ITSELF IF THEY BURN IT OUT OF THE SKY--

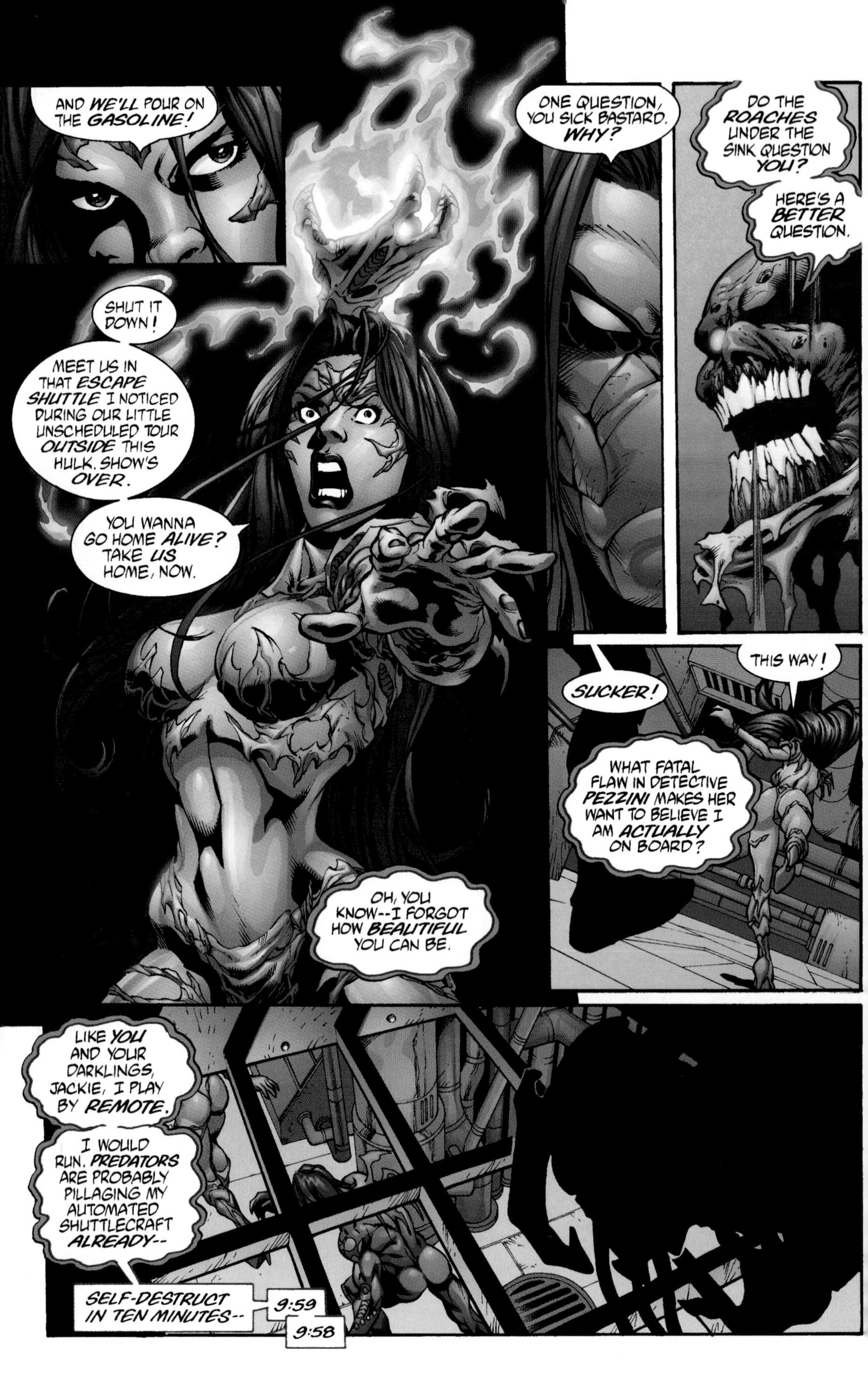
AND WE'LL POUR ON THE GASOLINE!
ONE QUESTION, YOU SICK BASTARD. WHY?
DO THE ROACHES UNDER THE SINK QUESTION YOU?
HERE'S A BETTER QUESTION.
SHUT IT DOWN!
MEET US IN THAT ESCAPE SHUTTLE I NOTICED DURING OUR LITTLE UNSCHEDULED TOUR OUTSIDE THIS HULK. SHOW'S OVER.
YOU WANNA GO HOME ALIVE? TAKE US HOME, NOW.
SUCKER!
THIS WAY!
WHAT FATAL FLAW IN DETECTIVE PEZZINI MAKES HER WANT TO BELIEVE I AM ACTUALLY ON BOARD?
OH, YOU KNOW--I FORGOT HOW BEAUTIFUL YOU CAN BE.
LIKE YOU AND YOUR DARKLINGS, JACKIE, I PLAY BY REMOTE.
I WOULD RUN. PREDATORS ARE PROBABLY PILLAGING MY AUTOMATED SHUTTLECRAFT ALREADY--
SELF-DESTRUCT IN TEN MINUTES--
9:59
9:58

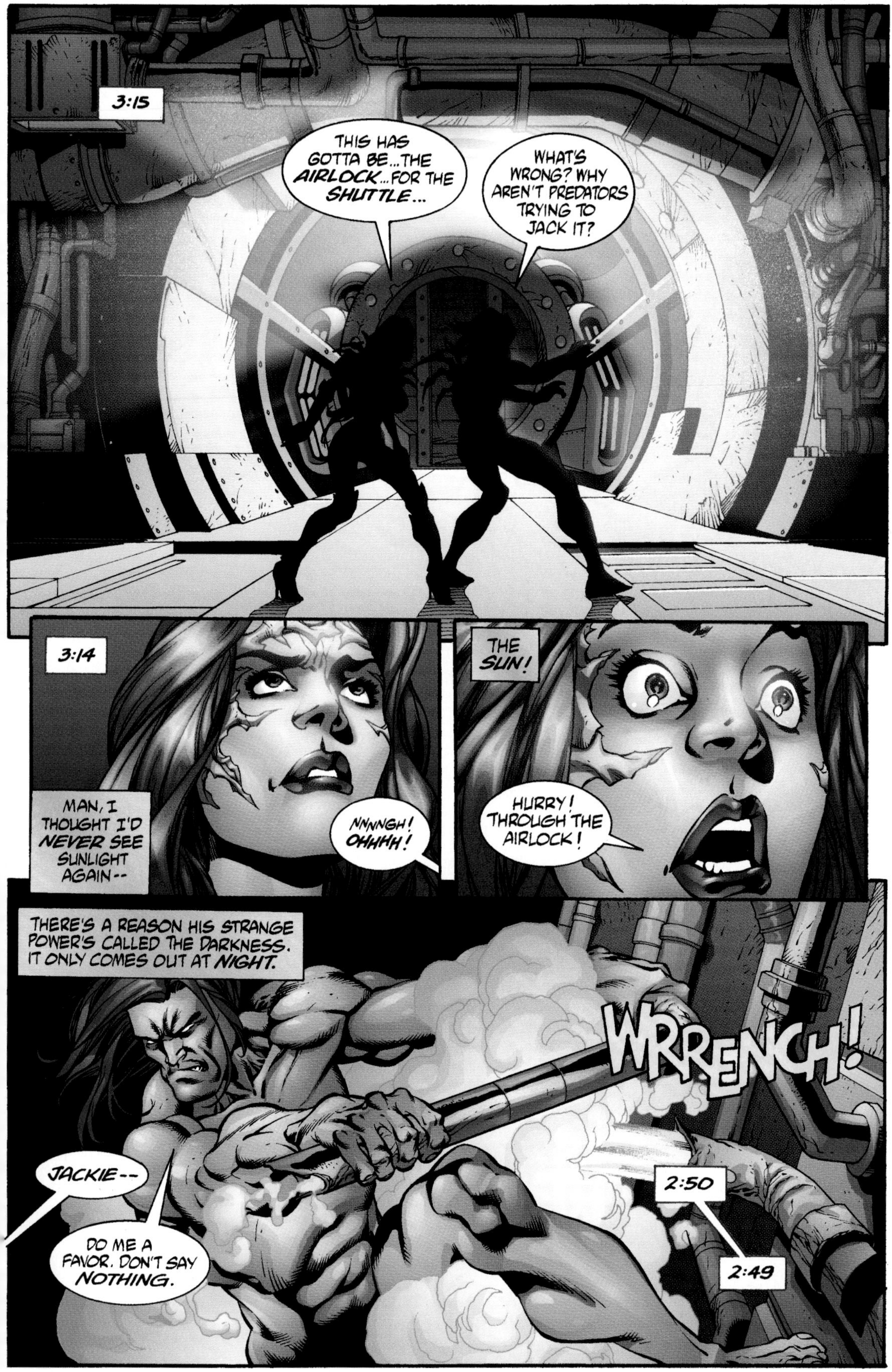
3:15
THIS HAS GOTTA BE...THE AIRLOCK...FOR THE SHUTTLE...
WHAT'S WRONG? WHY AREN'T PREDATORS TRYING TO JACK IT?
3:14
MAN, I THOUGHT I'D NEVER SEE SUNLIGHT AGAIN--
NNNNGH! OHHHH!
THE SUN!
HURRY! THROUGH THE AIRLOCK!
THERE'S A REASON HIS STRANGE POWER'S CALLED THE DARKNESS. IT ONLY COMES OUT AT NIGHT.
WRRENCH!
JACKIE--
DO ME A FAVOR. DON'T SAY NOTHING.
2:50
2:49

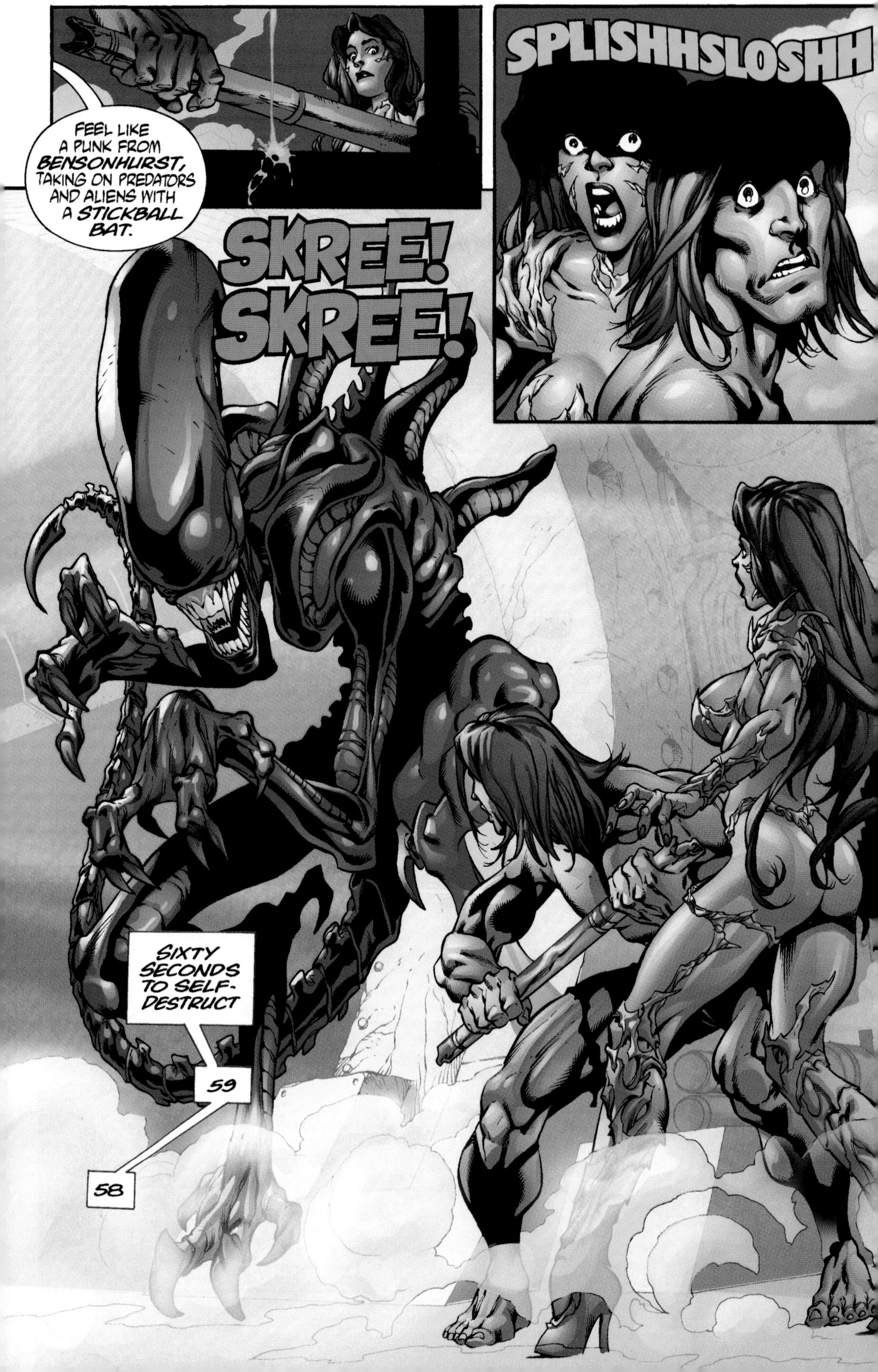
FEEL LIKE A PUNK FROM BENSONHURST, TAKING ON PREDATORS AND ALIENS WITH A STICKBALL BAT.
SPLISHHSLOSHH
SKREE! SKREE!
SIXTY SECONDS TO SELF-DESTRUCT
59
58

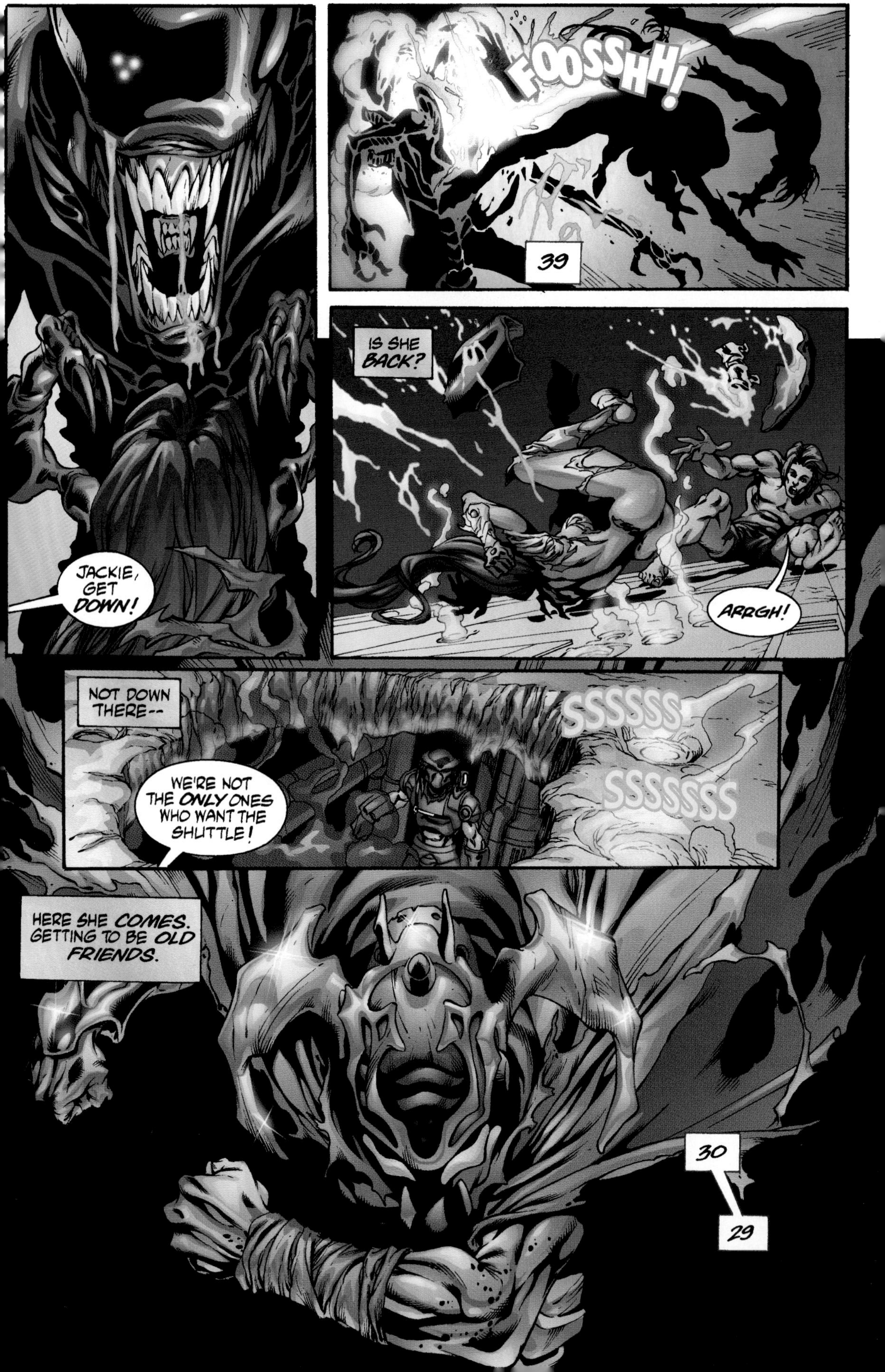
FOOSSHH!
39
JACKIE, GET DOWN!
IS SHE BACK?
ARRGH!
NOT DOWN THERE--
SSSSSS
SSSSSSS
WE'RE NOT THE ONLY ONES WHO WANT THE SHUTTLE!
HERE SHE COMES. GETTING TO BE OLD FRIENDS.
30
29

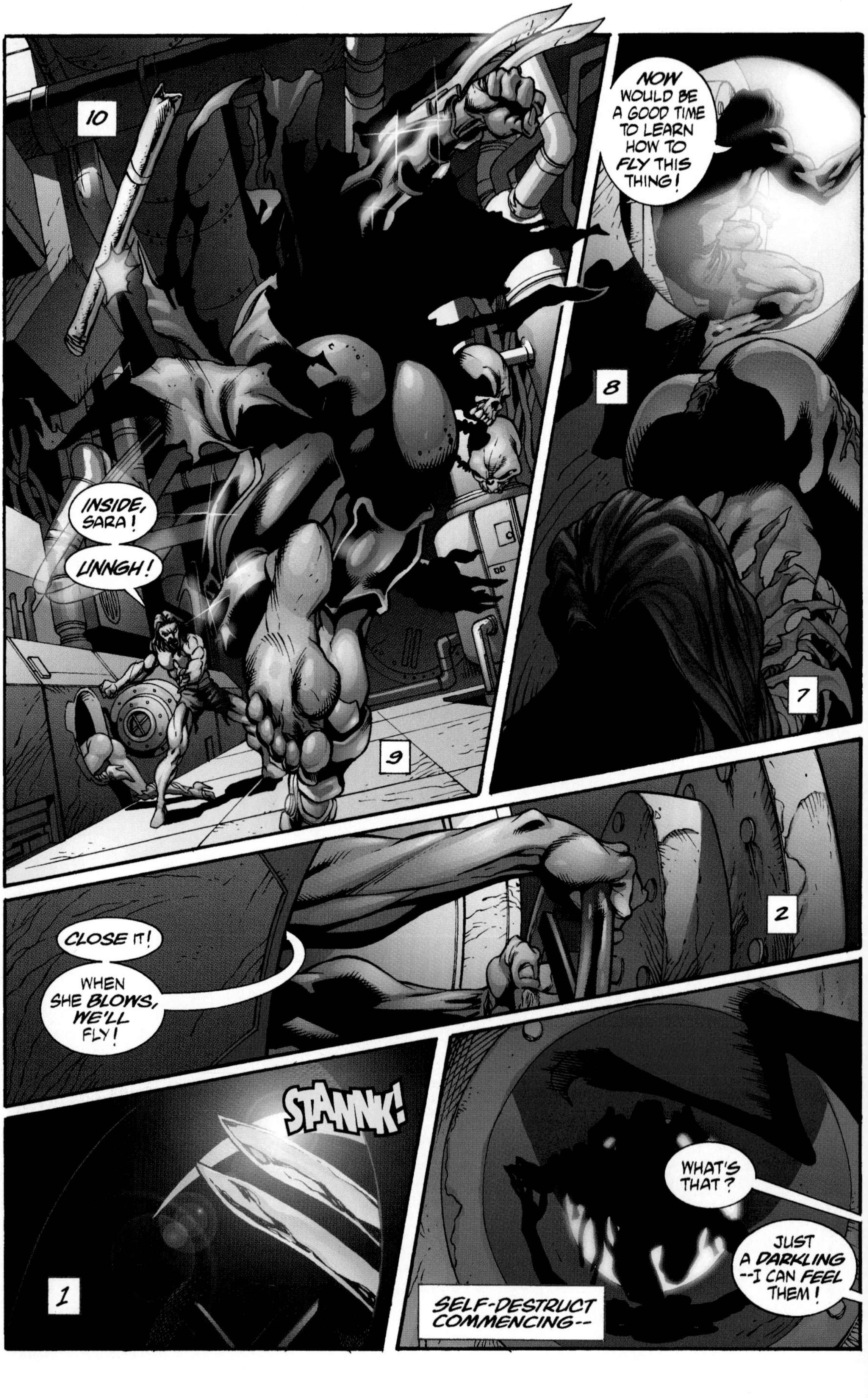
1
STANNK!
SELF-DESTRUCT COMMENCING--
WHAT'S THAT?
JUST A DARKLING --I CAN FEEL THEM!
2
CLOSE IT!
WHEN SHE BLOWS, WE'LL FLY!
7
8
NOW WOULD BE A GOOD TIME TO LEARN HOW TO FLY THIS THING!
9
10
INSIDE, SARA!
UNNGH!

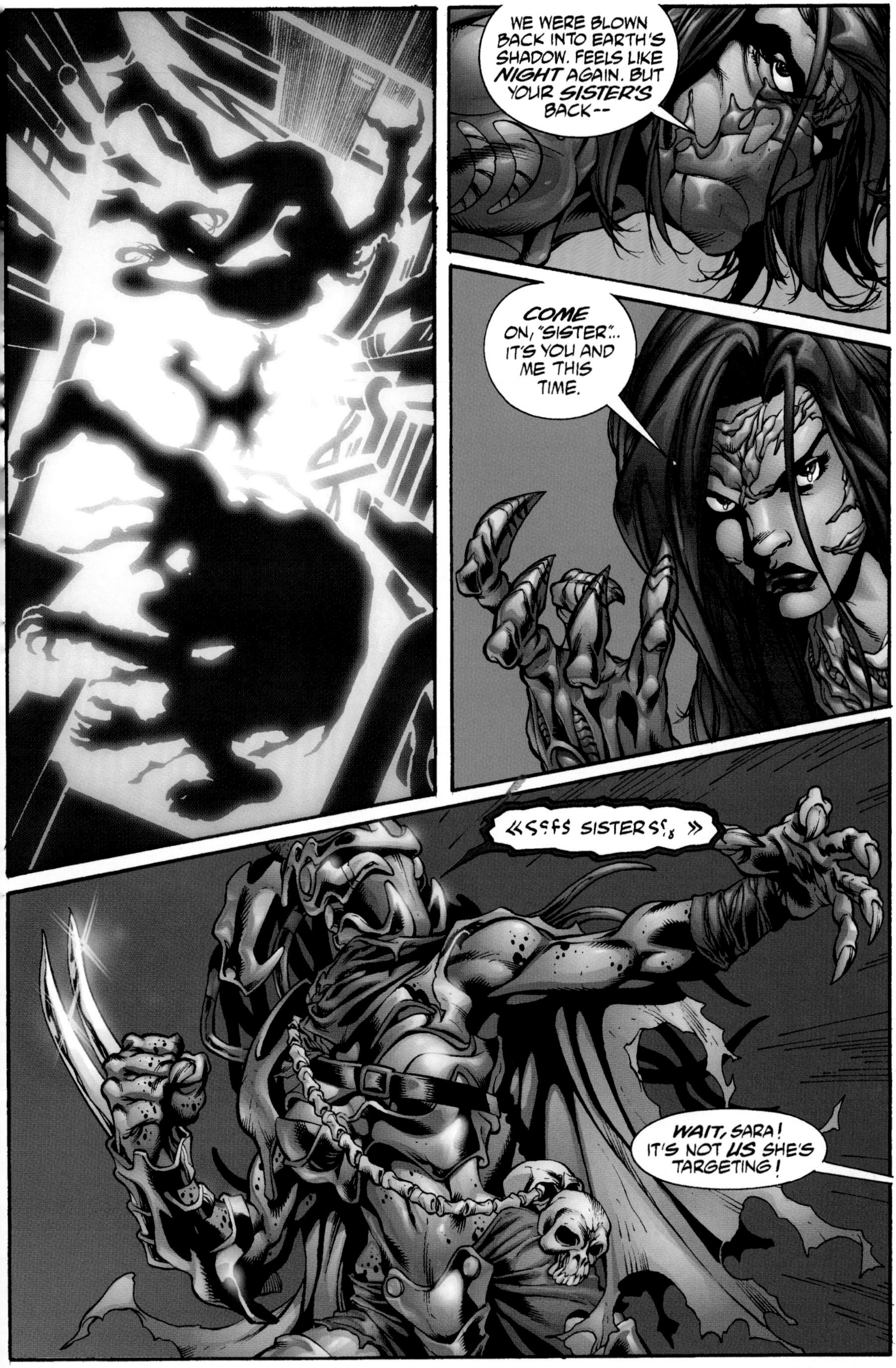
WE WERE BLOWN BACK INTO EARTH'S SHADOW. FEELS LIKE NIGHT AGAIN. BUT YOUR SISTER'S BACK--
COME ON, "SISTER"... IT'S YOU AND ME THIS TIME.
WAIT, SARA! IT'S NOT US SHE'S TARGETING!

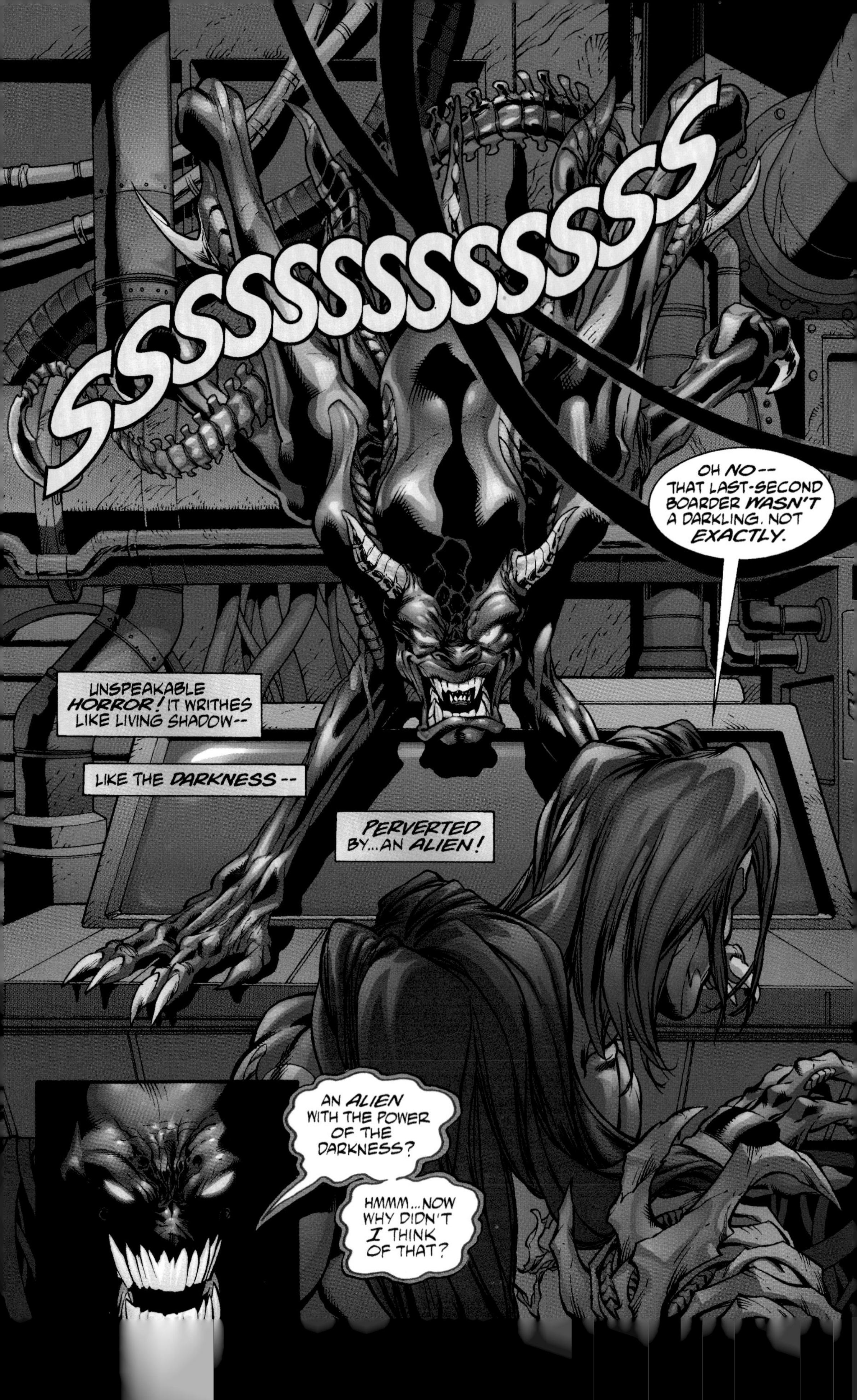
SSSSSSSSSSSSS
OH NO-- THAT LAST-SECOND BOARDER WASN'T A DARKLING. NOT EXACTLY.
UNSPEAKABLE HORROR! IT WRITHES LIKE LIVING SHADOW--
LIKE THE DARKNESS--
PERVERTED BY...AN ALIEN!
AN ALIEN WITH THE POWER OF THE DARKNESS?
HMMM...NOW WHY DIDN'T I THINK OF THAT?

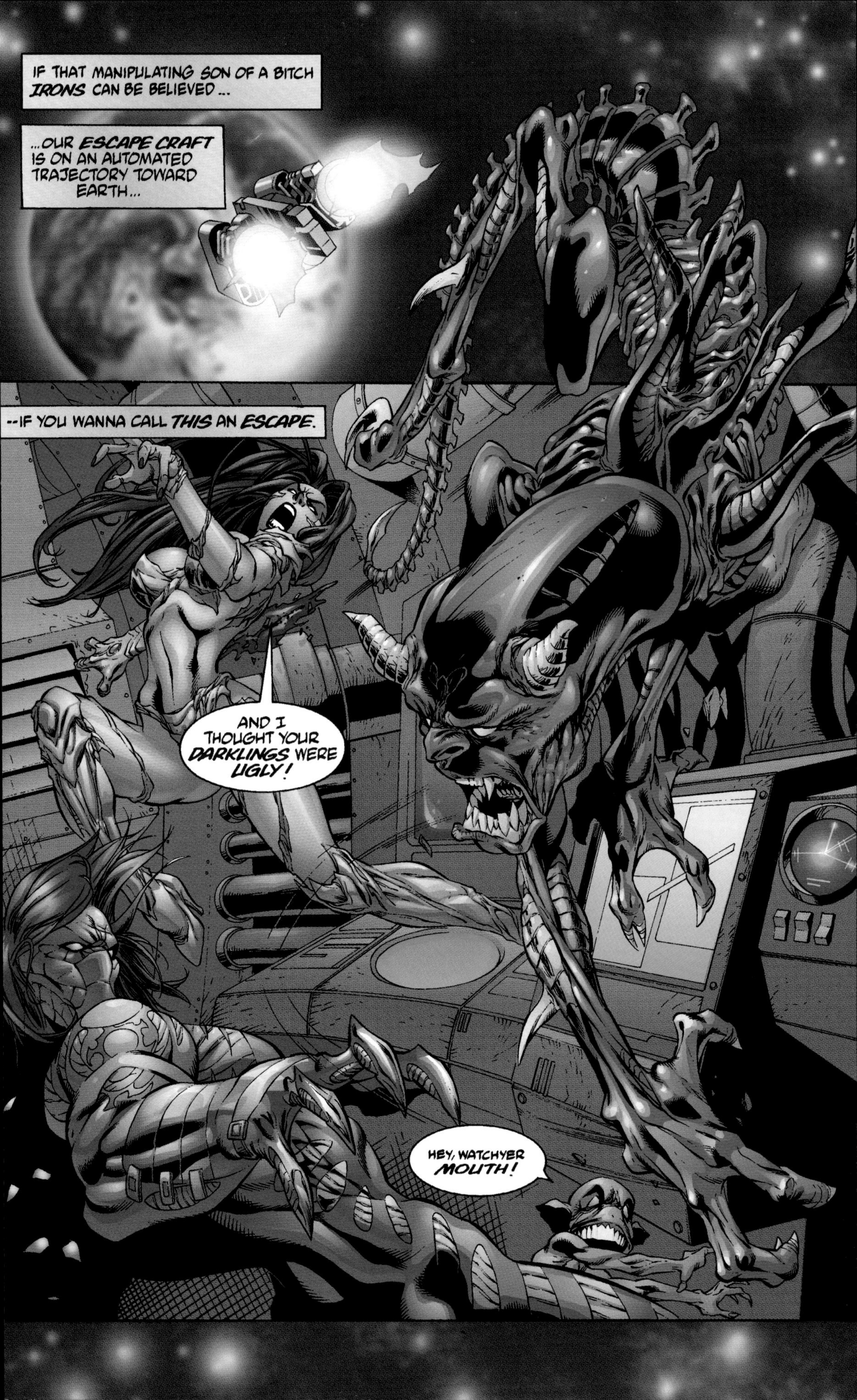
IF THAT MANIPULATING SON OF A BITCH IRONS CAN BE BELIEVED...
...OUR ESCAPE CRAFT IS ON AN AUTOMATED TRAJECTORY TOWARD EARTH...
--IF YOU WANNA CALL THIS AN ESCAPE.
AND I THOUGHT YOUR DARKLINGS WERE UGLY!
HEY, WATCHYER MOUTH!

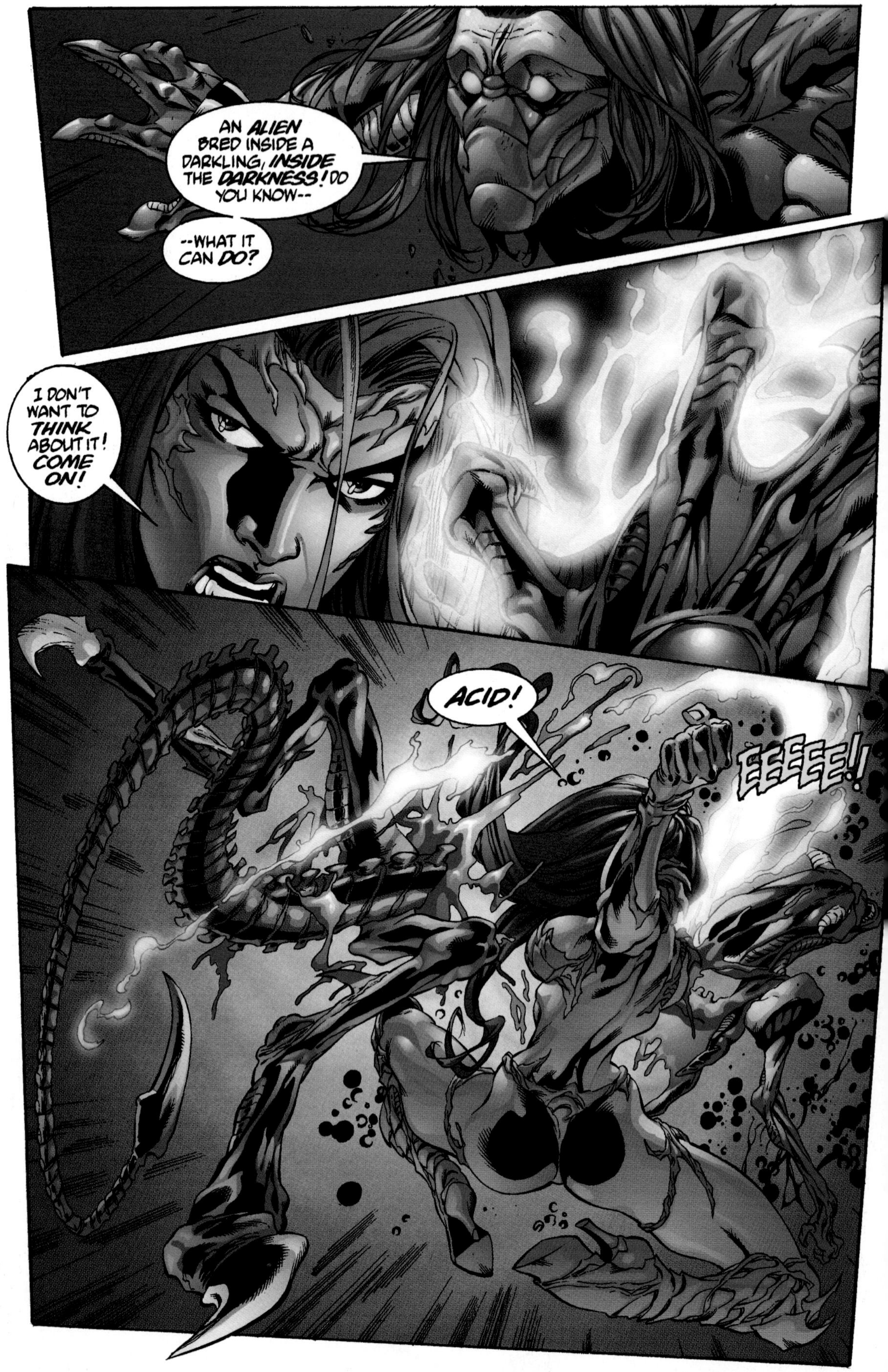
AN ALIEN BRED INSIDE A DARKLING, INSIDE THE DARKNESS! DO YOU KNOW--
--WHAT IT CAN DO?
I DON'T WANT TO THINK ABOUT IT! COME ON!
ACID!
EEEEE!!

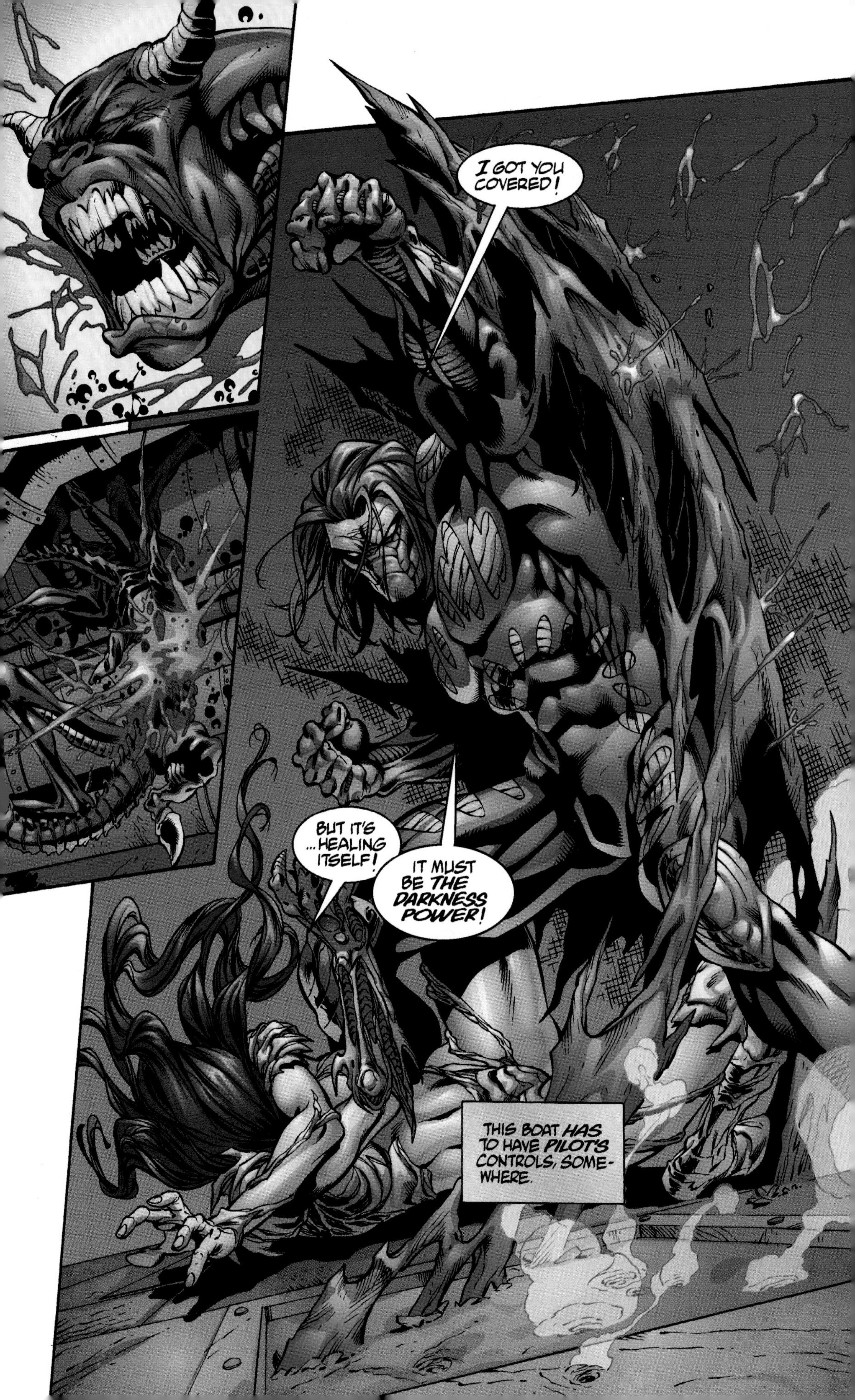
I GOT YOU COVERED!
BUT IT'S ...HEALING ITSELF!
IT MUST BE THE DARKNESS POWER!
THIS BOAT HAS TO HAVE PILOT'S CONTROLS, SOMEWHERE.

CREEP

HEY! CHECK IT OUT.

SHE HAS HER EYE ON THE *WITCH-BLADE*.

CREEP

TELL HER IT'S NOT FOR *SALE*.

GFYSKZ

HUH?!

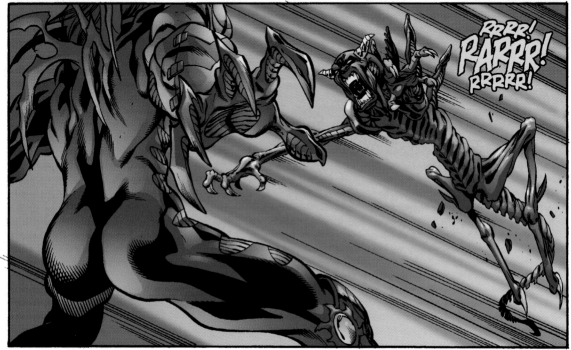

RRRR! RARRR! RRRRR!

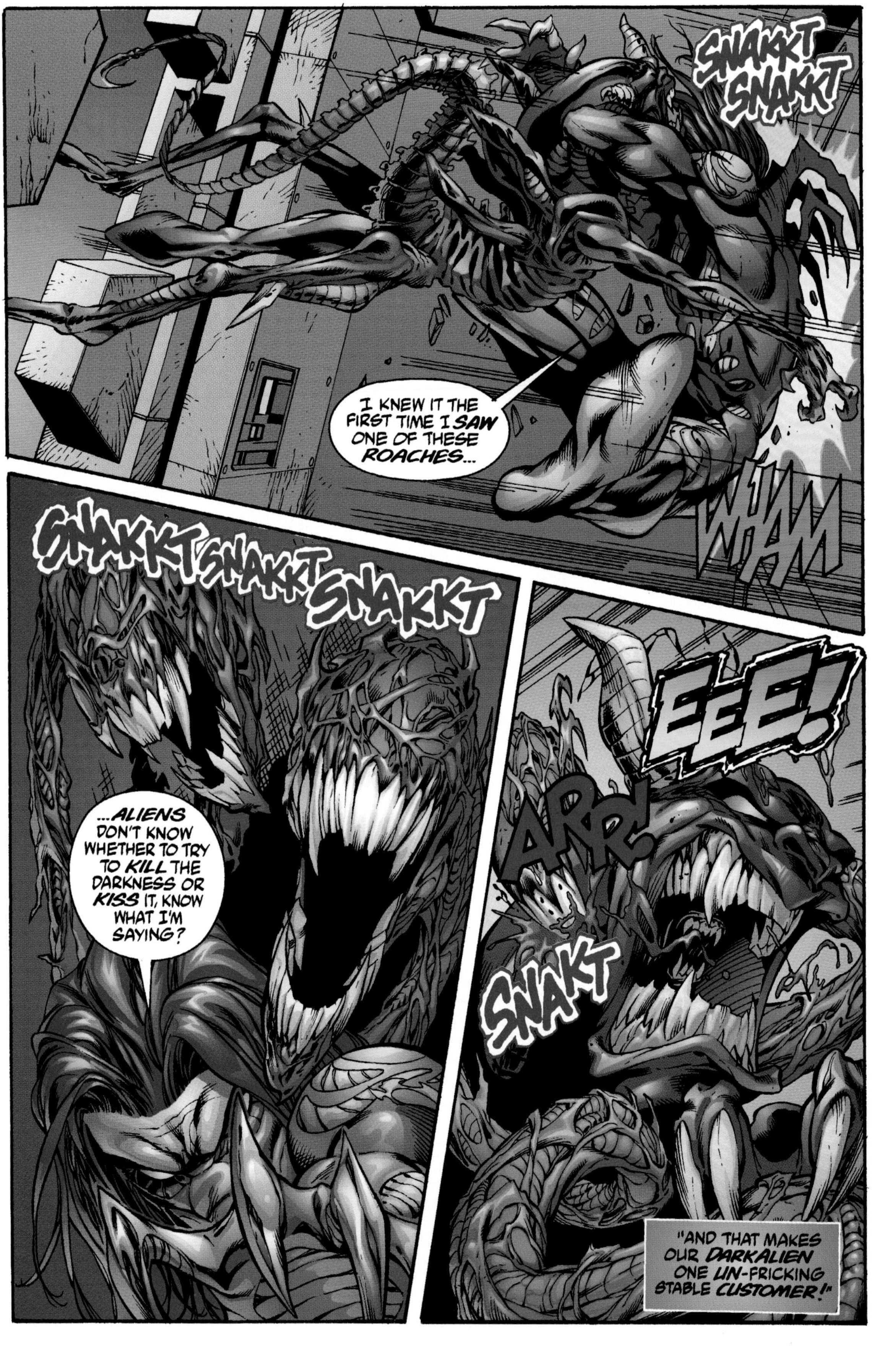
SNAKKT SNAKKT
I KNEW IT THE FIRST TIME I SAW ONE OF THESE ROACHES...
WHAM
SNAKKT SNAKKT SNAKKT
...ALIENS DON'T KNOW WHETHER TO TRY TO KILL THE DARKNESS OR KISS IT, KNOW WHAT I'M SAYING?
EEE!
ARR!
SNAKT
"AND THAT MAKES OUR DARKALIEN ONE UN-FRICKING STABLE CUSTOMER!"

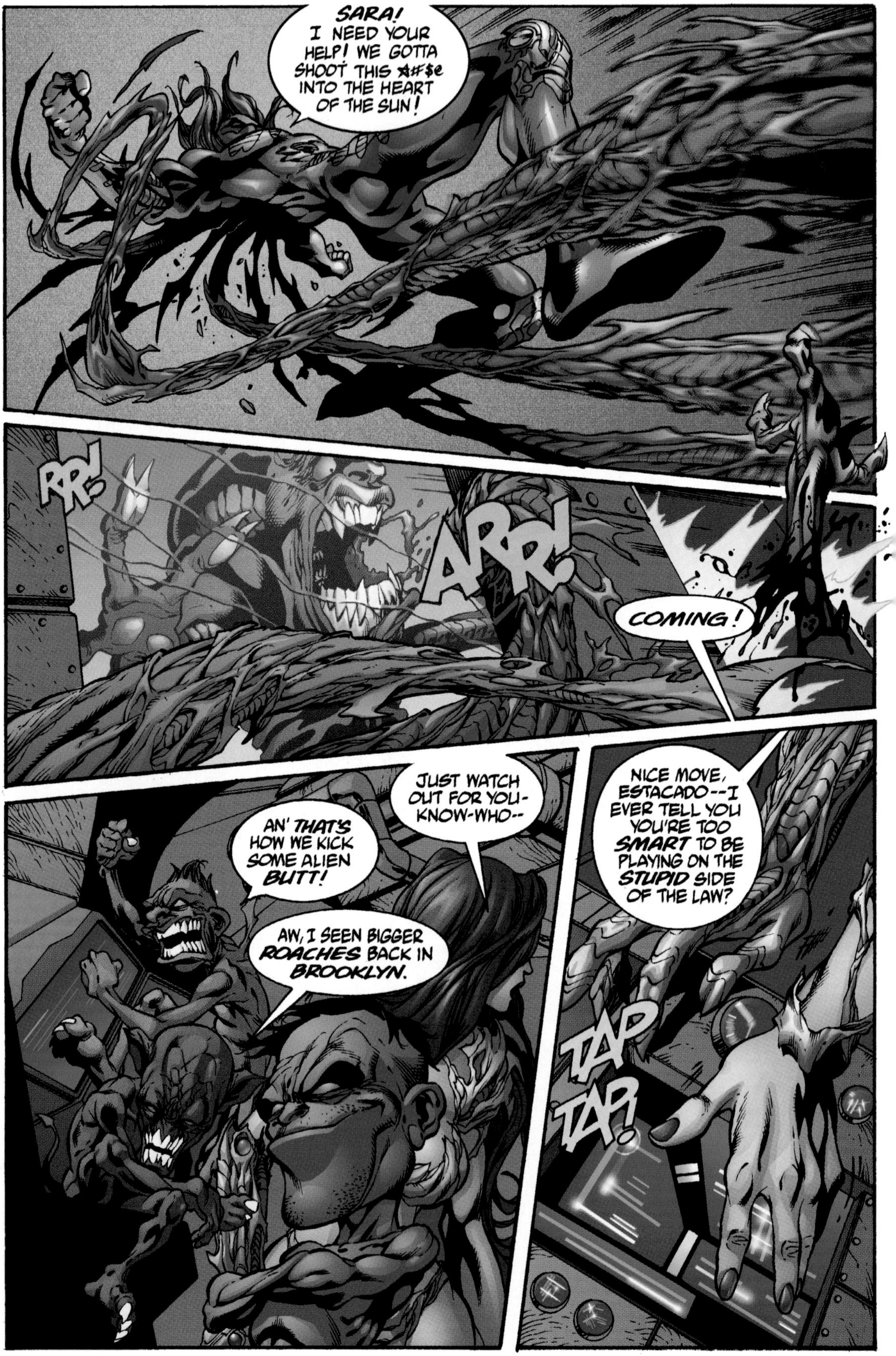
SARA! I NEED YOUR HELP! WE GOTTA SHOOT THIS $@#$e INTO THE HEART OF THE SUN!
RR!
ARR!
COMING!
AN' THAT'S HOW WE KICK SOME ALIEN BUTT!
JUST WATCH OUT FOR YOU-KNOW-WHO--
AW, I SEEN BIGGER ROACHES BACK IN BROOKLYN.
NICE MOVE, ESTACADO--I EVER TELL YOU YOU'RE TOO SMART TO BE PLAYING ON THE STUPID SIDE OF THE LAW?
TAP
TAP!

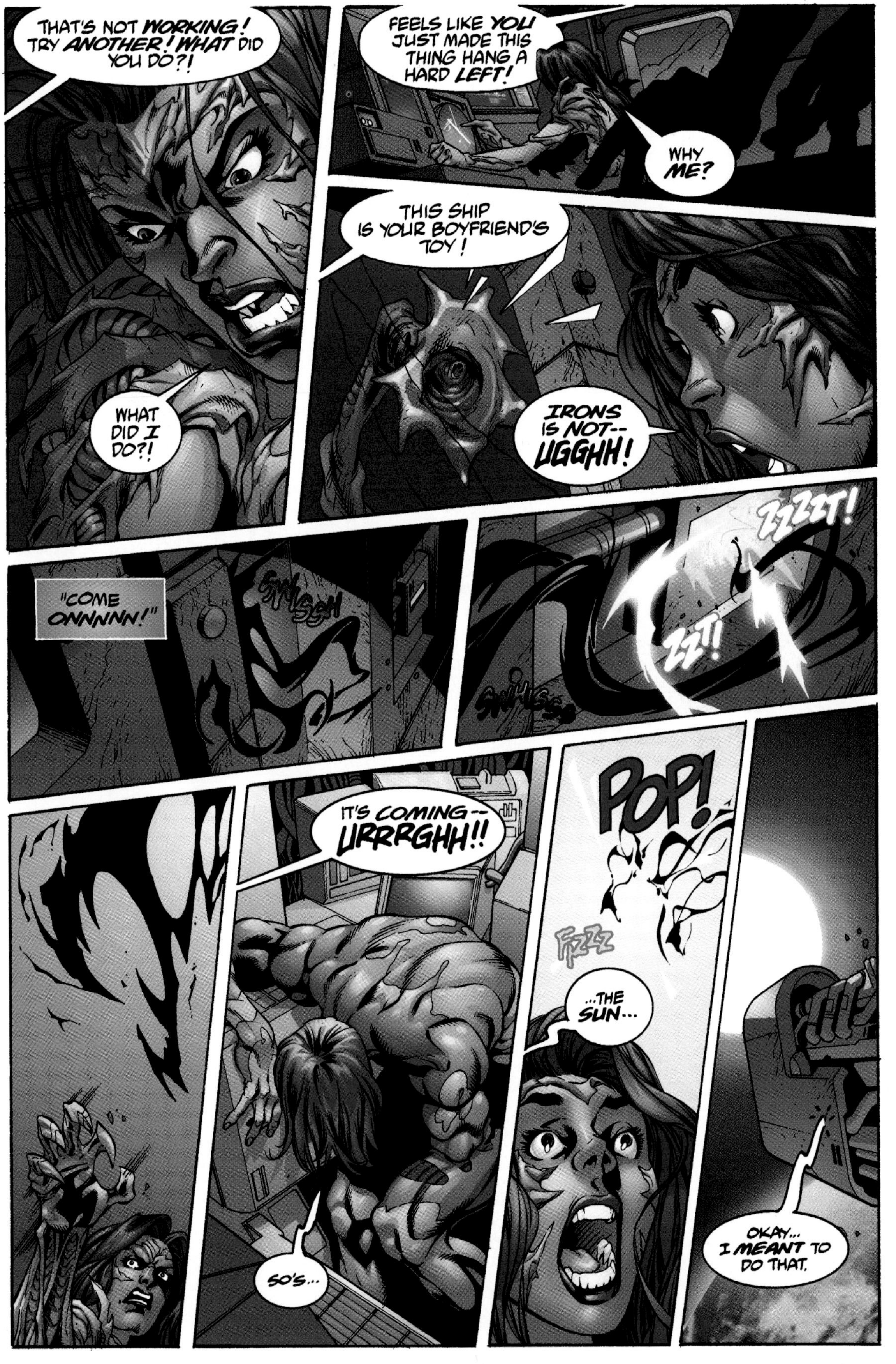
THAT'S NOT WORKING! TRY ANOTHER! WHAT DID YOU DO?!
FEELS LIKE YOU JUST MADE THIS THING HANG A HARD LEFT!
WHY ME?
THIS SHIP IS YOUR BOYFRIEND'S TOY!
WHAT DID I DO?!
IRONS IS NOT-- UGGHH!
"COME ONNNNN!"
SHLUSSH
ZZZZT!
ZZT!
SHHUSSS
IT'S COMING-- URRRGHH!!
SO'S...
POP!
FZZZ
...THE SUN...
OKAY... I MEANT TO DO THAT.

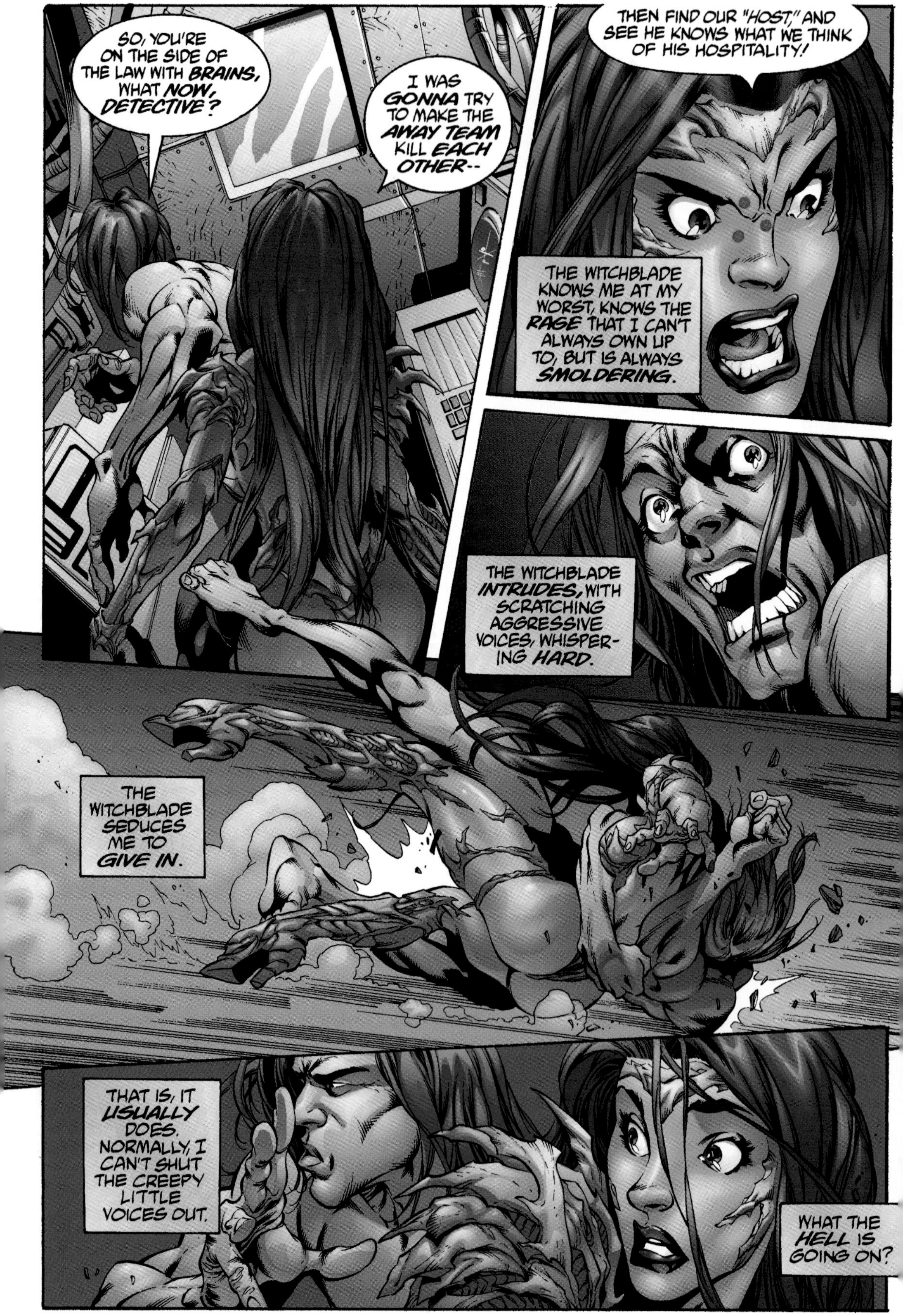

SO, YOU'RE ON THE SIDE OF THE LAW WITH BRAINS, WHAT NOW, DETECTIVE?
I WAS GONNA TRY TO MAKE THE AWAY TEAM KILL EACH OTHER--
THEN FIND OUR "HOST," AND SEE HE KNOWS WHAT WE THINK OF HIS HOSPITALITY!
THE WITCHBLADE KNOWS ME AT MY WORST, KNOWS THE RAGE THAT I CAN'T ALWAYS OWN UP TO, BUT IS ALWAYS SMOLDERING.
THE WITCHBLADE INTRUDES, WITH SCRATCHING AGGRESSIVE VOICES, WHISPERING HARD.
THE WITCHBLADE SEDUCES ME TO GIVE IN.
THAT IS, IT USUALLY DOES. NORMALLY, I CAN'T SHUT THE CREEPY LITTLE VOICES OUT.
WHAT THE HELL IS GOING ON?

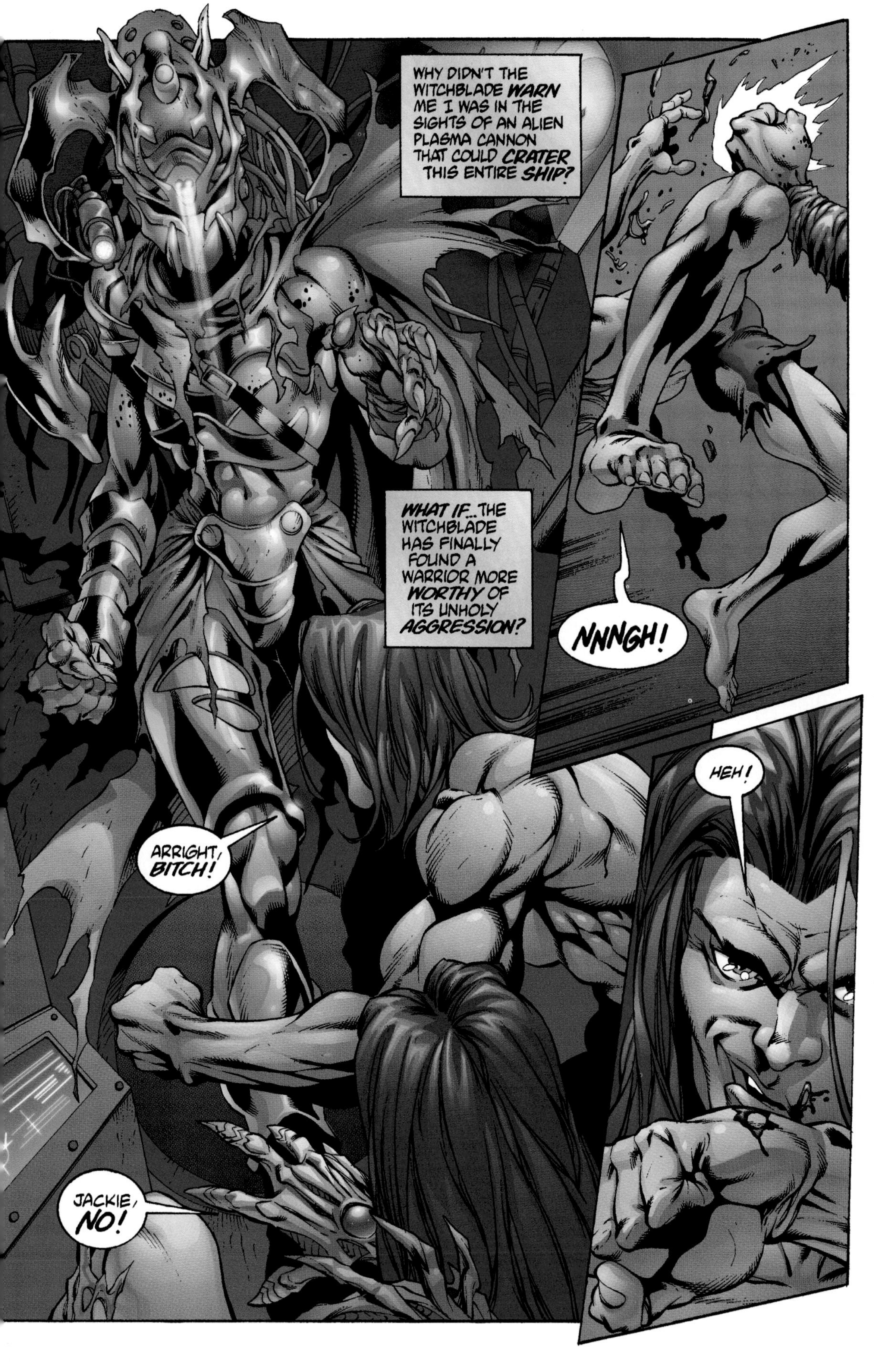

WHY DIDN'T THE WITCHBLADE WARN ME I WAS IN THE SIGHTS OF AN ALIEN PLASMA CANNON THAT COULD CRATER THIS ENTIRE SHIP?
WHAT IF... THE WITCHBLADE HAS FINALLY FOUND A WARRIOR MORE WORTHY OF ITS UNHOLY AGGRESSION?
NNNGH!
ARRIGHT, BITCH!
HEH!
JACKIE, NO!

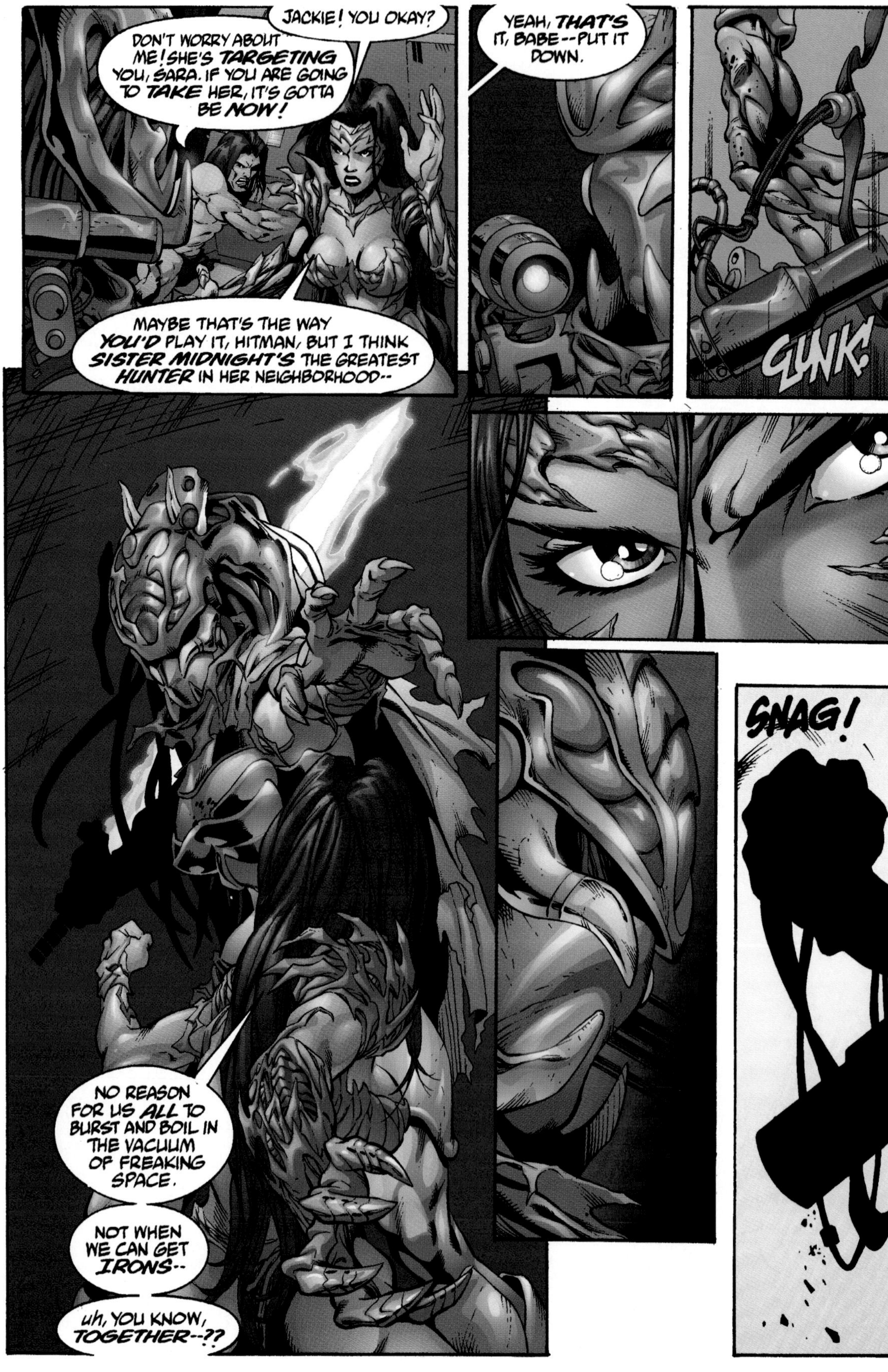
JACKIE! YOU OKAY?
DON'T WORRY ABOUT ME! SHE'S TARGETING YOU, SARA. IF YOU ARE GOING TO TAKE HER, IT'S GOTTA BE NOW!
MAYBE THAT'S THE WAY YOU'D PLAY IT, HITMAN, BUT I THINK SISTER MIDNIGHT'S THE GREATEST HUNTER IN HER NEIGHBORHOOD--
YEAH, THAT'S IT, BABE--PUT IT DOWN.
CLUNK!
NO REASON FOR US ALL TO BURST AND BOIL IN THE VACUUM OF FREAKING SPACE.
NOT WHEN WE CAN GET IRONS--
uh, YOU KNOW, TOGETHER--??
SNAG!

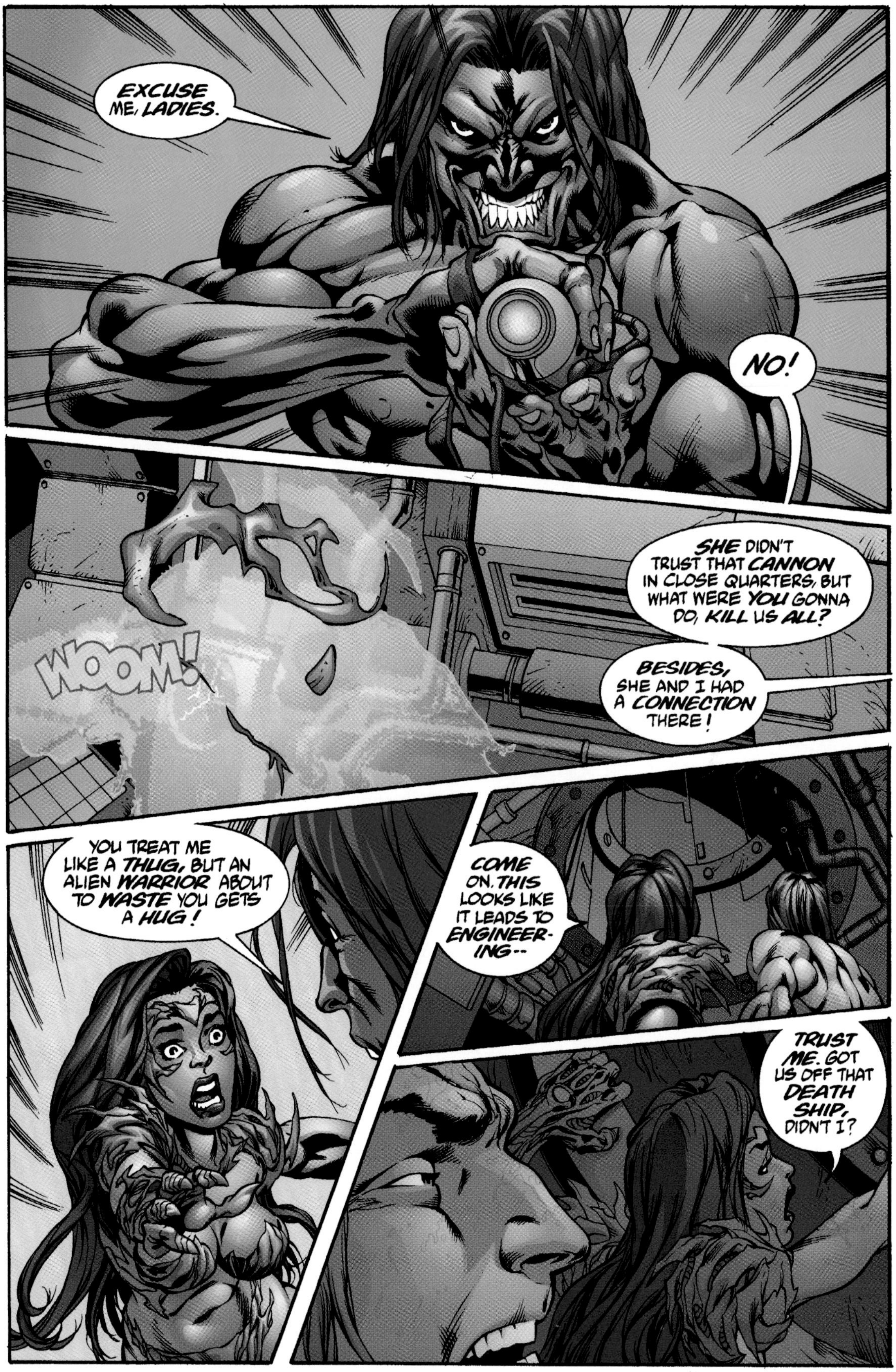
EXCUSE ME, LADIES.
NO!
WOOM!
SHE DIDN'T TRUST THAT CANNON IN CLOSE QUARTERS, BUT WHAT WERE YOU GONNA DO, KILL US ALL?
BESIDES, SHE AND I HAD A CONNECTION THERE!
YOU TREAT ME LIKE A THUG, BUT AN ALIEN WARRIOR ABOUT TO WASTE YOU GETS A HUG!
COME ON. THIS LOOKS LIKE IT LEADS TO ENGINEER-ING--
TRUST ME. GOT US OFF THAT DEATH SHIP, DIDN'T I?

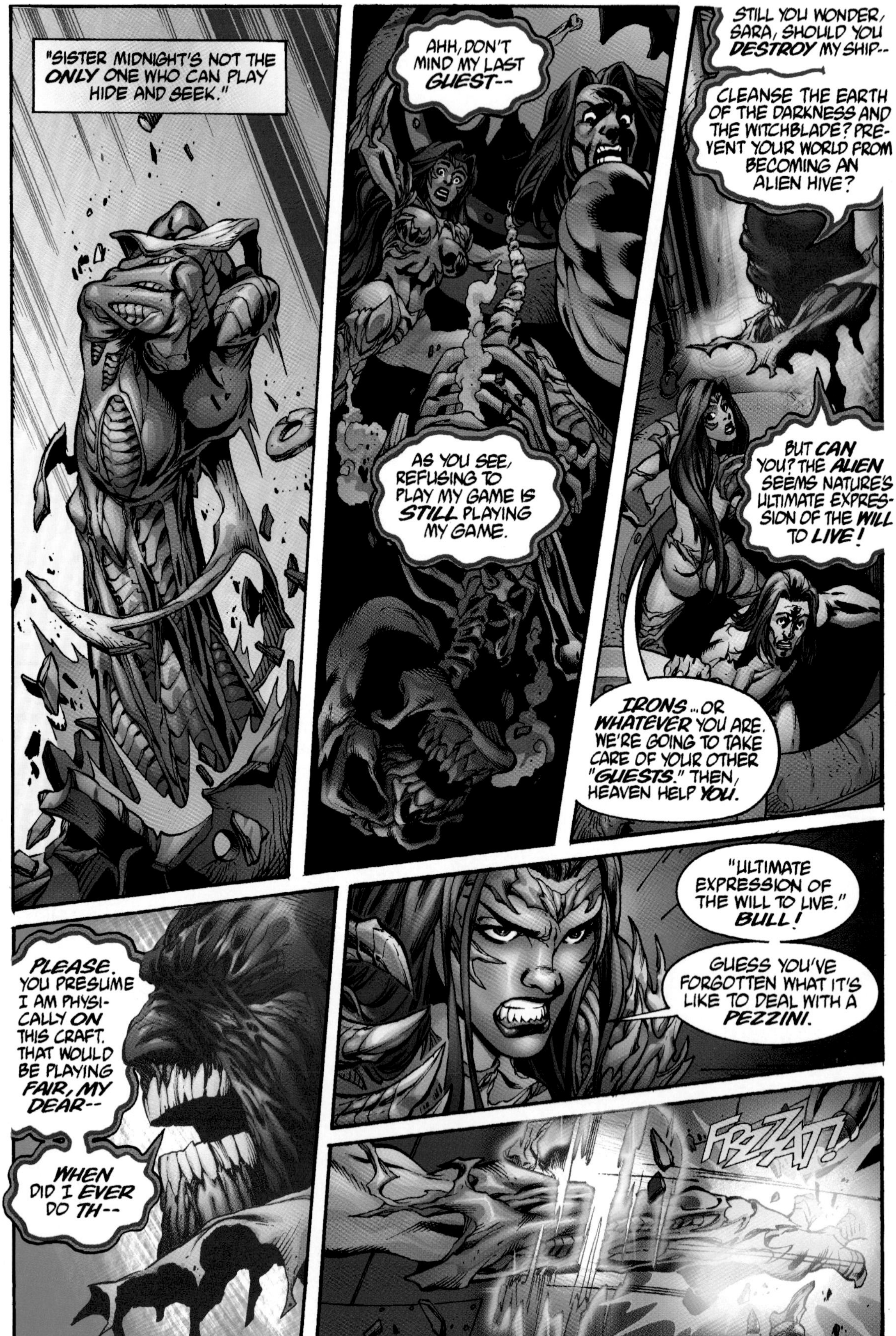
"SISTER MIDNIGHT'S NOT THE ONLY ONE WHO CAN PLAY HIDE AND SEEK."
AHH, DON'T MIND MY LAST GUEST--
AS YOU SEE, REFUSING TO PLAY MY GAME IS STILL PLAYING MY GAME.
STILL YOU WONDER, SARA, SHOULD YOU DESTROY MY SHIP--
CLEANSE THE EARTH OF THE DARKNESS AND THE WITCHBLADE? PRE-VENT YOUR WORLD FROM BECOMING AN ALIEN HIVE?
BUT CAN YOU? THE ALIEN SEEMS NATURE'S ULTIMATE EXPRES-SION OF THE WILL TO LIVE!
IRONS...OR WHATEVER YOU ARE. WE'RE GOING TO TAKE CARE OF YOUR OTHER "GUESTS." THEN, HEAVEN HELP YOU.
PLEASE. YOU PRESUME I AM PHYSI-CALLY ON THIS CRAFT. THAT WOULD BE PLAYING FAIR, MY DEAR--
WHEN DID I EVER DO TH--
"ULTIMATE EXPRESSION OF THE WILL TO LIVE." BULL!
GUESS YOU'VE FORGOTTEN WHAT IT'S LIKE TO DEAL WITH A PEZZINI.
FRZZAT!

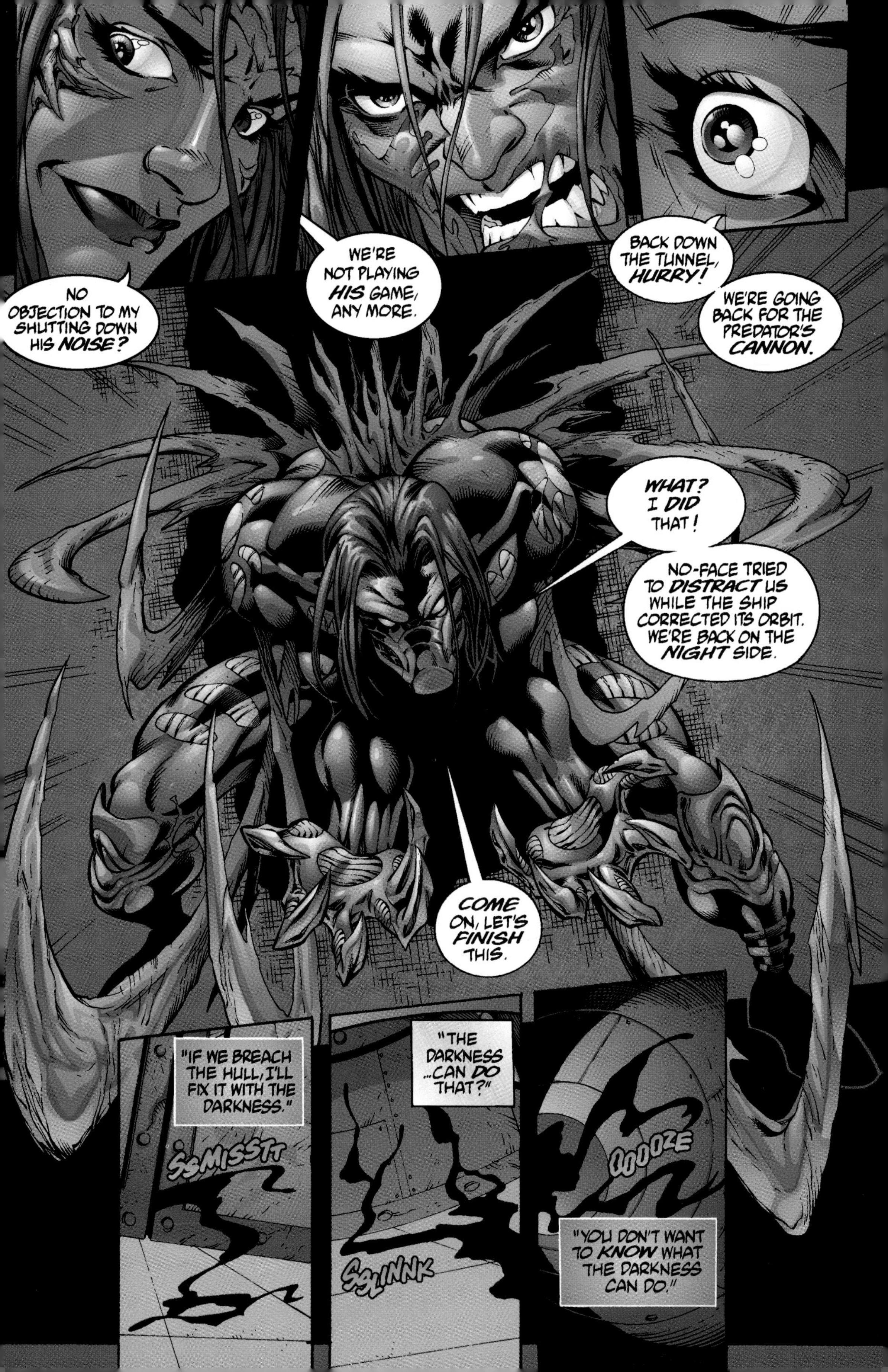
NO OBJECTION TO MY SHUTTING DOWN HIS NOISE?
WE'RE NOT PLAYING HIS GAME, ANY MORE.
BACK DOWN THE TUNNEL, HURRY!
WE'RE GOING BACK FOR THE PREDATOR'S CANNON.
WHAT? I DID THAT!
NO-FACE TRIED TO DISTRACT US WHILE THE SHIP CORRECTED ITS ORBIT. WE'RE BACK ON THE NIGHT SIDE.
COME ON, LET'S FINISH THIS.
"IF WE BREACH THE HULL, I'LL FIX IT WITH THE DARKNESS."
SSMISSTT
"THE DARKNESS ...CAN DO THAT?"
SSLINNK
OOOOZE
"YOU DON'T WANT TO KNOW WHAT THE DARKNESS CAN DO."

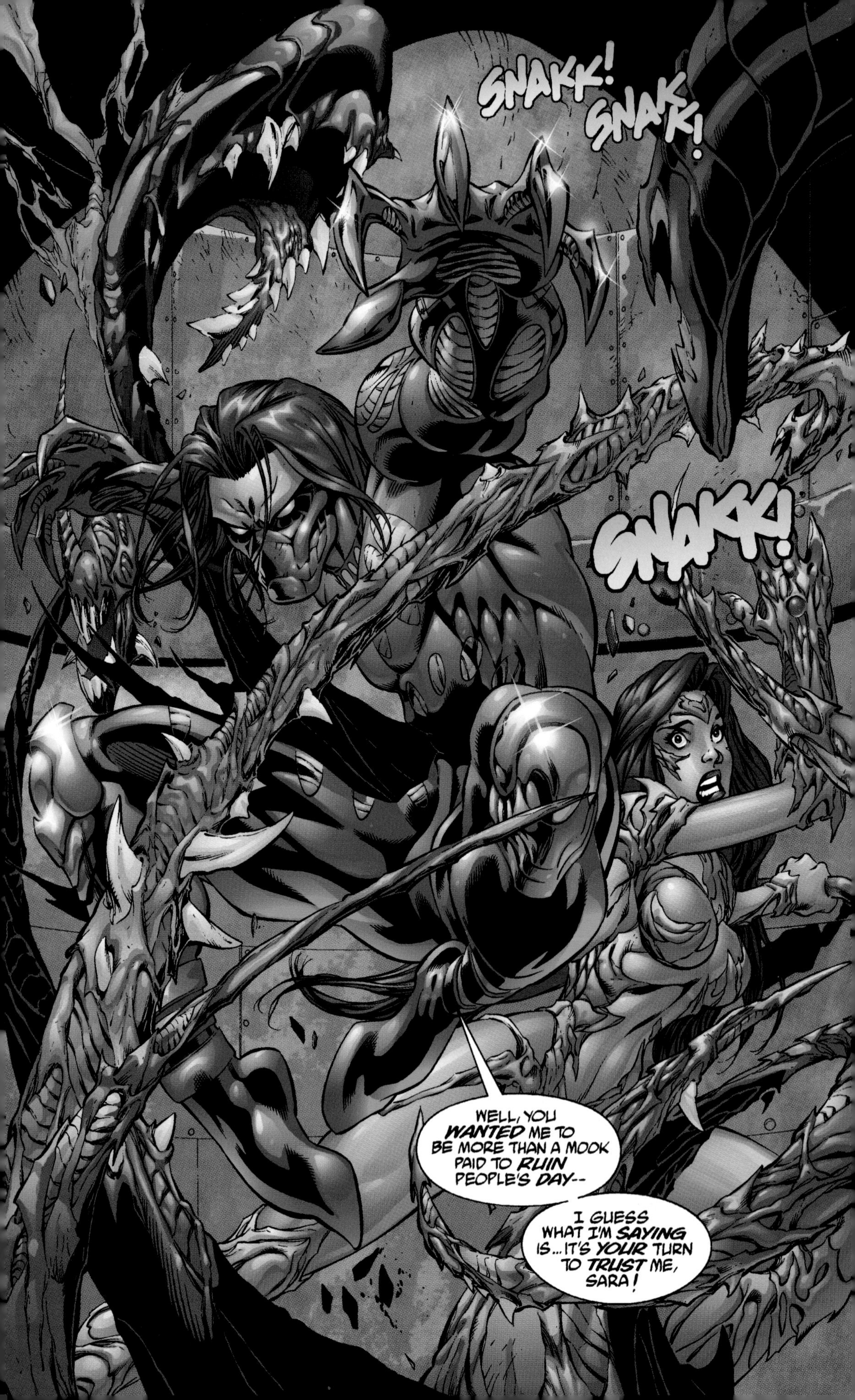
SNAKK! SNAKK!
SNAKK!
WELL, YOU WANTED ME TO BE MORE THAN A MOOK PAID TO RUIN PEOPLE'S DAY--
I GUESS WHAT I'M SAYING IS...IT'S YOUR TURN TO TRUST ME, SARA!

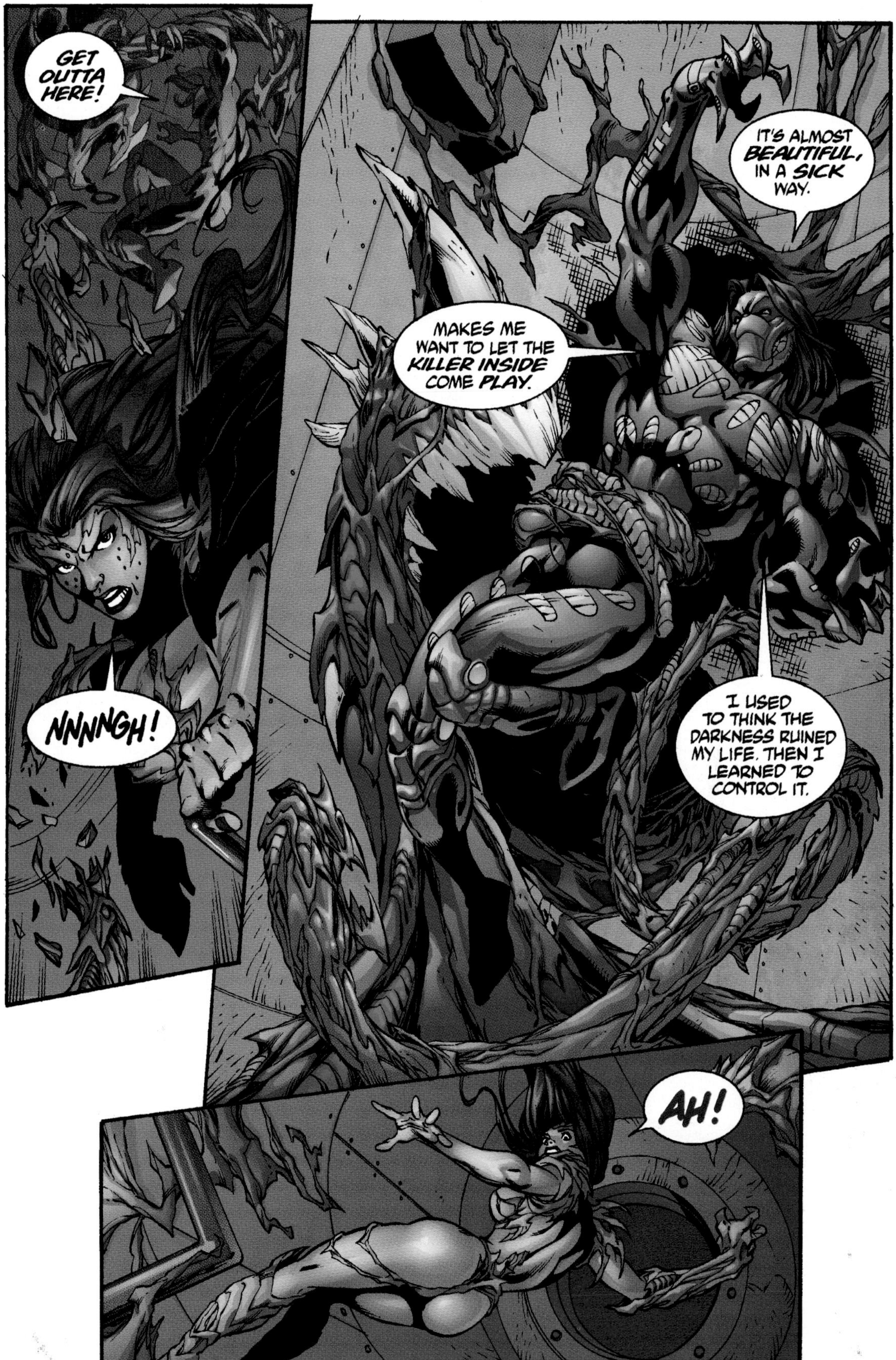
GET OUTTA HERE!
NNNNGH!
IT'S ALMOST BEAUTIFUL, IN A SICK WAY.
MAKES ME WANT TO LET THE KILLER INSIDE COME PLAY.
I USED TO THINK THE DARKNESS RUINED MY LIFE. THEN I LEARNED TO CONTROL IT.
AH!

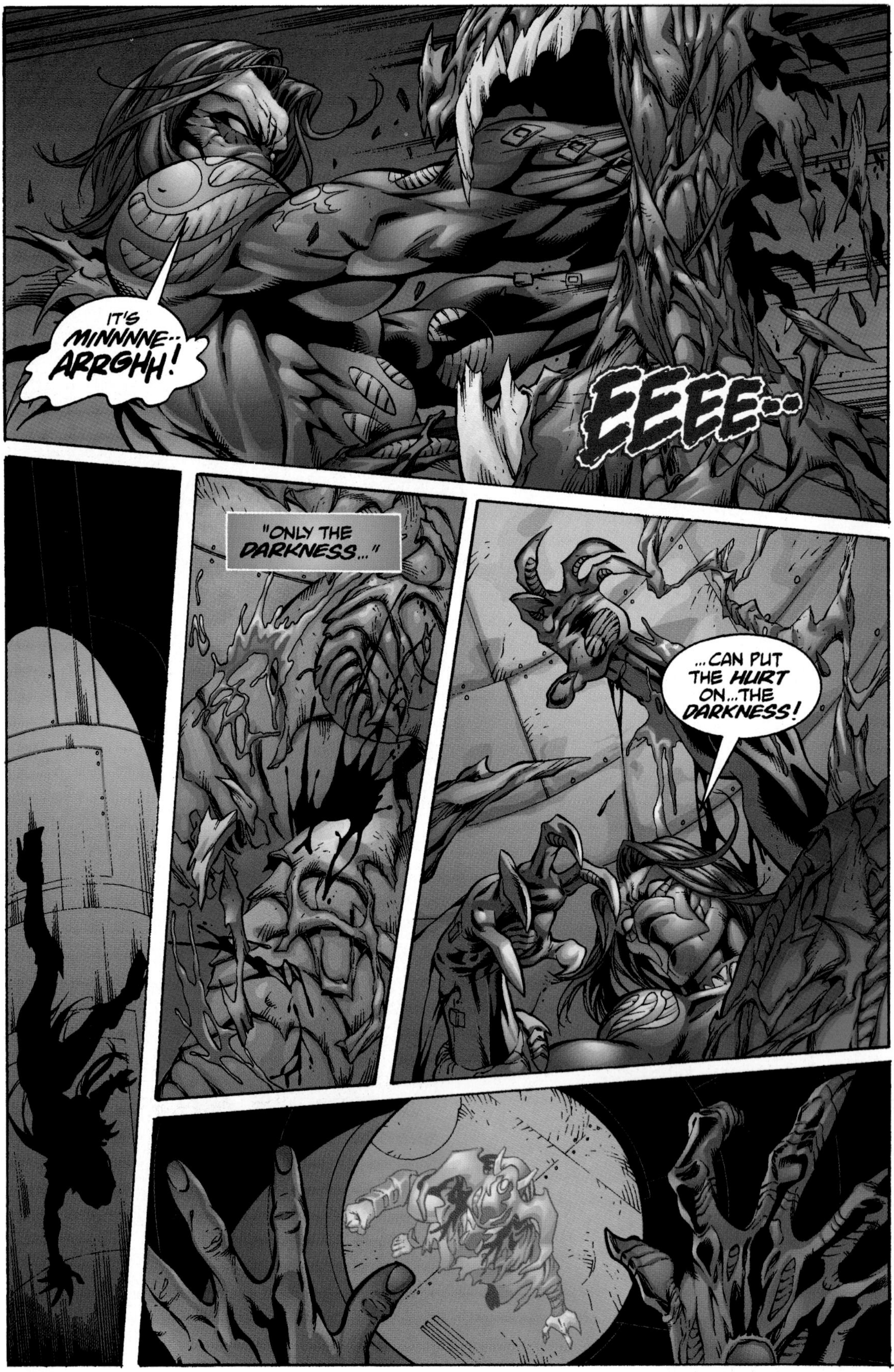

IT'S MINNNNE... ARRGHH!
EEEE...
"ONLY THE DARKNESS..."
...CAN PUT THE HURT ON...THE DARKNESS!

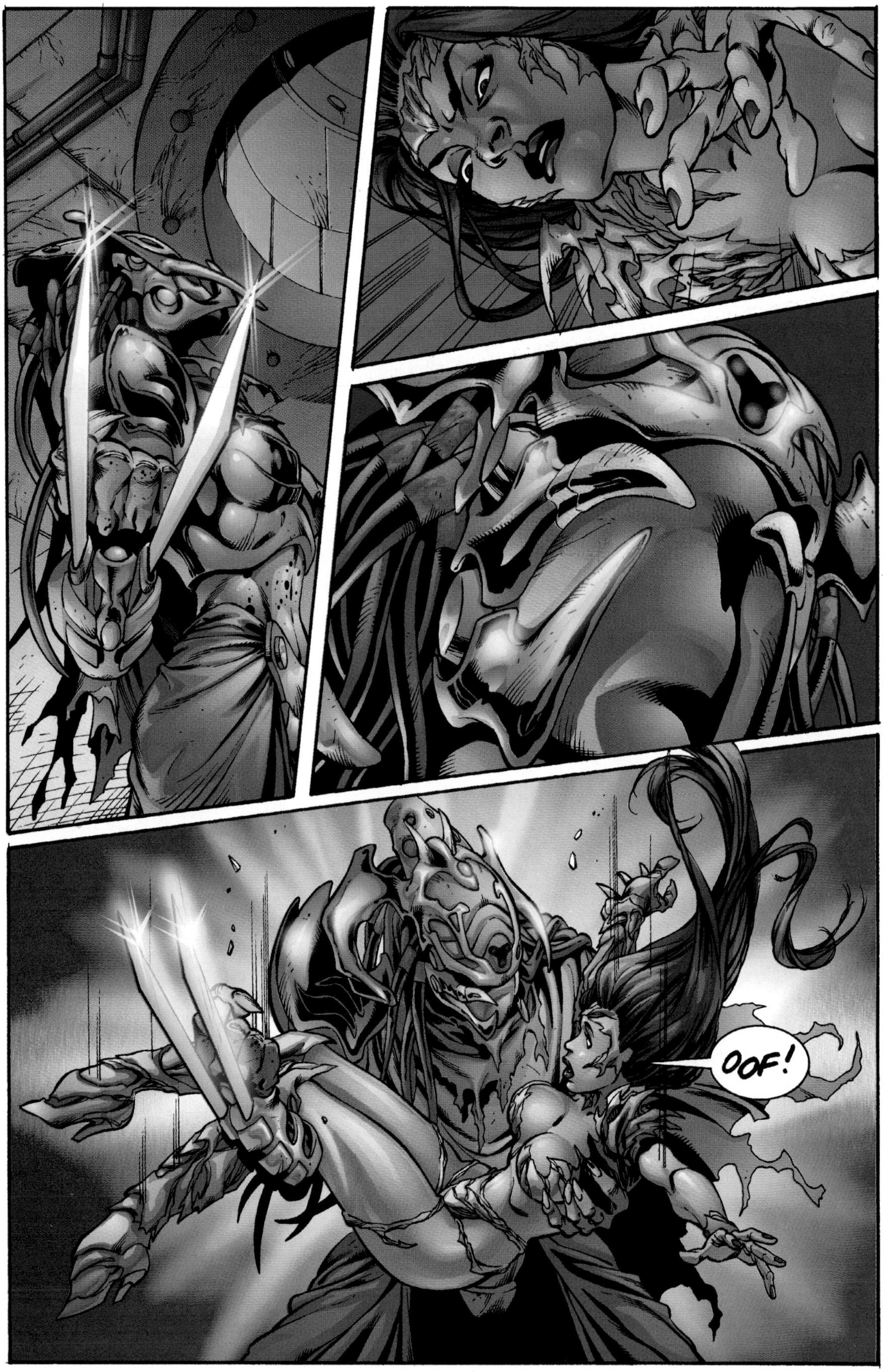
OOF!

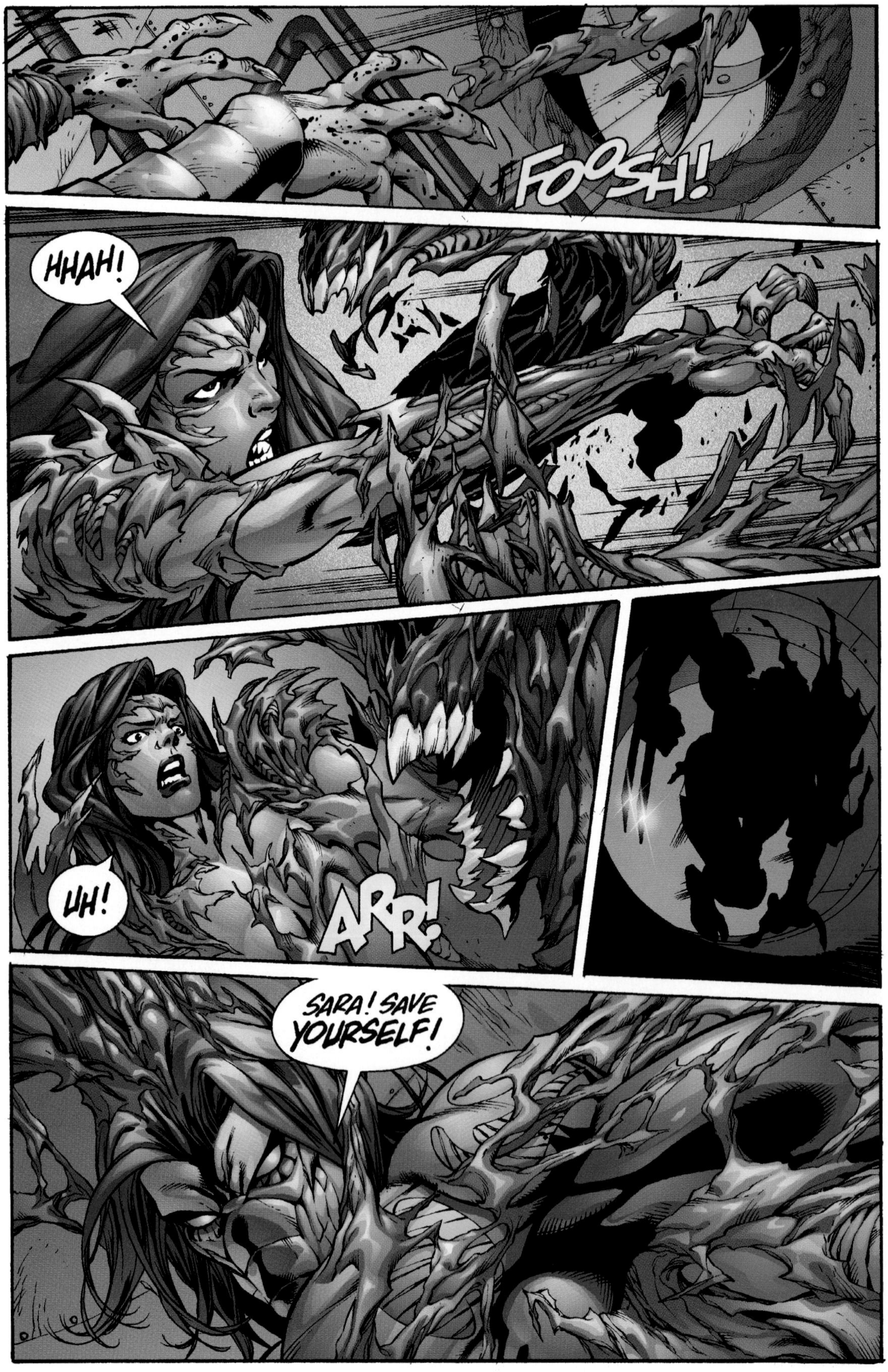
FOOSH!
HHAH!
UH!
ARR!
SARA! SAVE YOURSELF!

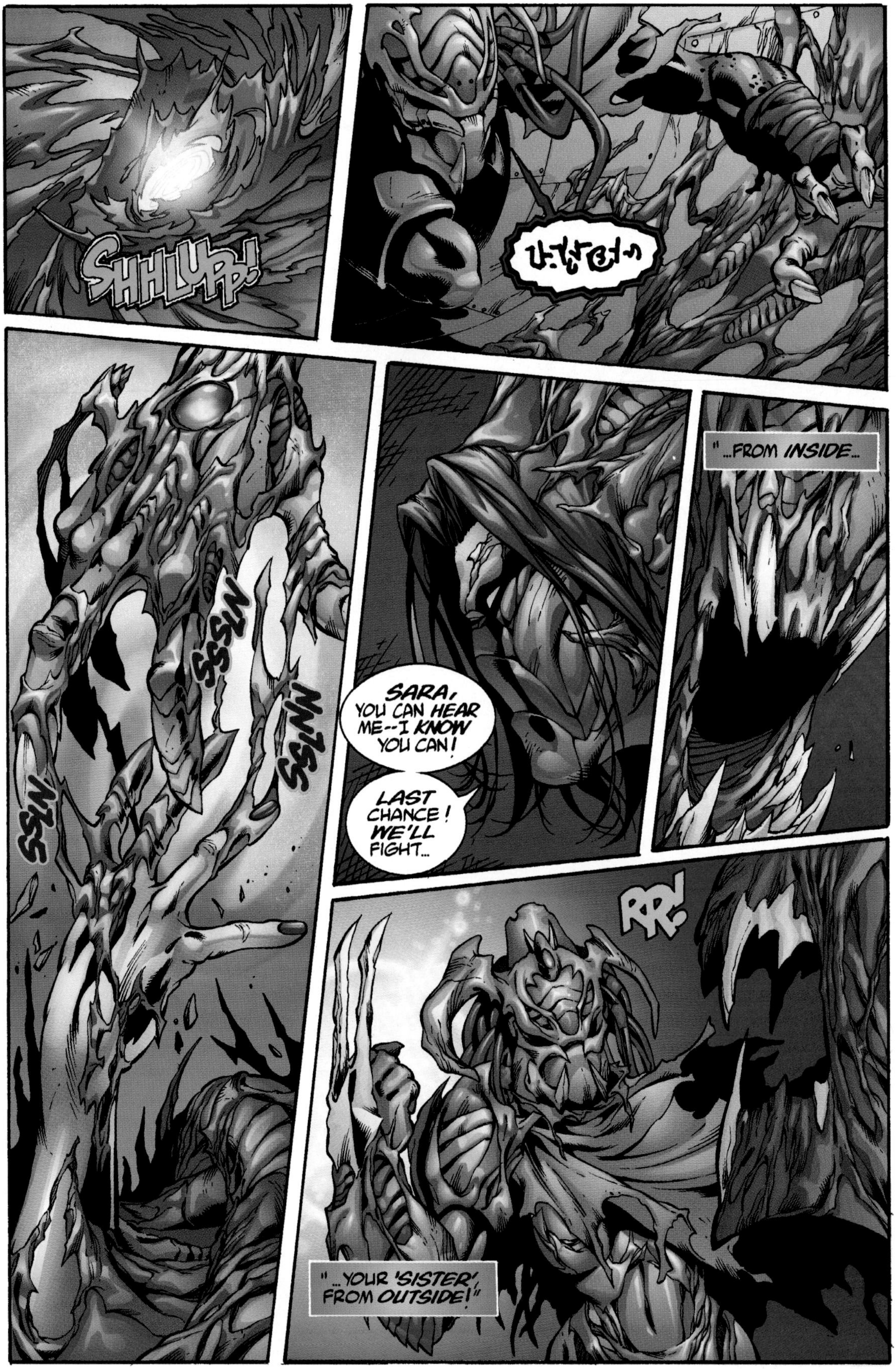
SHHLUPP!
SARA, YOU CAN HEAR ME--I KNOW YOU CAN!
LAST CHANCE! WE'LL FIGHT...
"...FROM INSIDE...
RR!
"...YOUR 'SISTER', FROM OUTSIDE!"

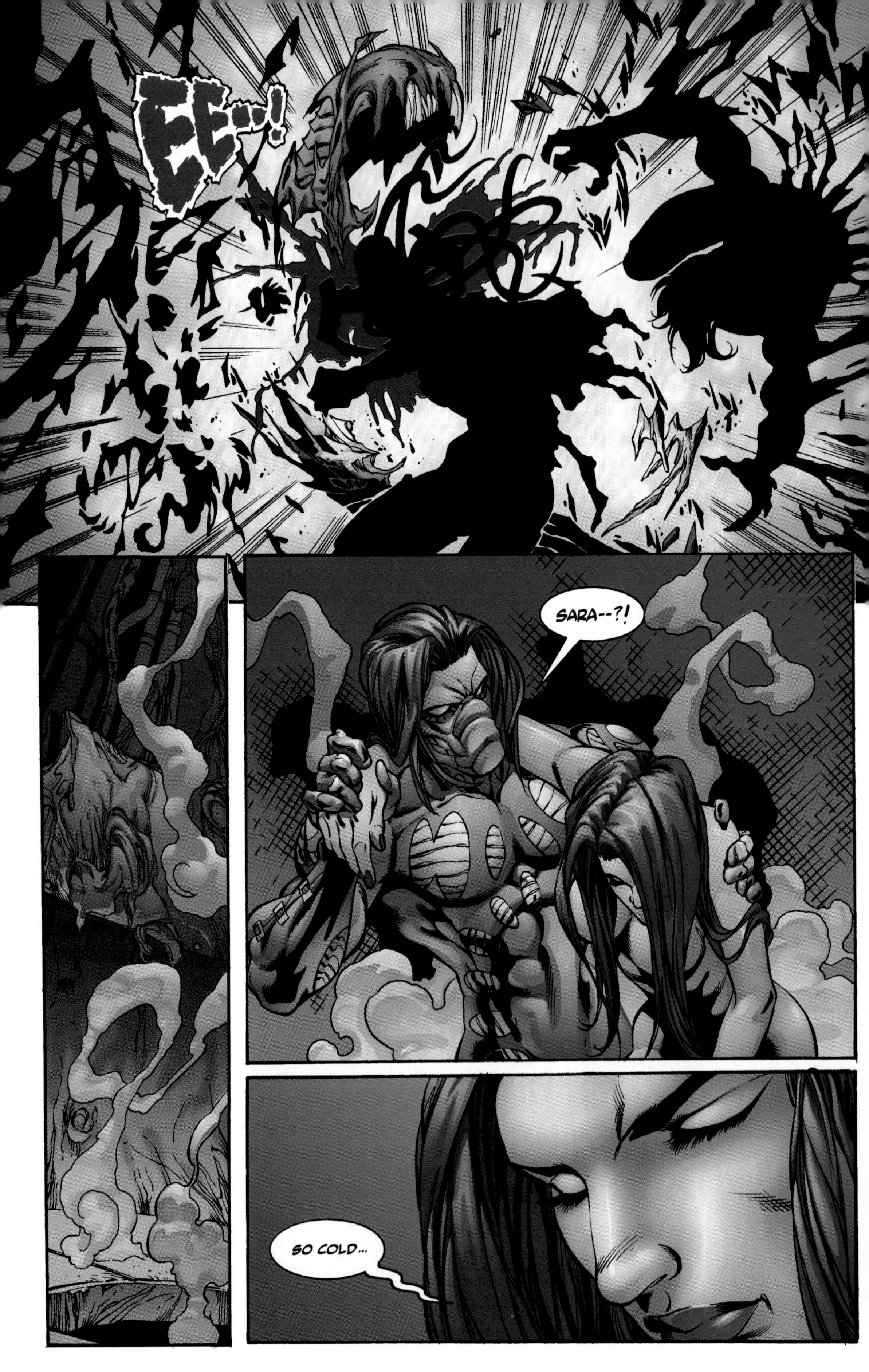
EE...!
SARA--?!
SO COLD...

A *COP* COULD DO *WORSE* THAN DYING ON HER WATCH-- *YOU* WOULD KNOW, *RIGHT,* DAD?

WE GOT THE *BAD GUY,* ONE MORE TIME. AND I DON'T FEEL BAD. I'M COMING HOME TO *YOLI.*

JACKIE MIGHT NOT *GET* IT. HE'S BEEN ON THE WRONG SIDE FOR TOO LONG. SO I DON'T TELL *HIM.*

BUT I KNOW SISTER MIDNIGHT.

SHE GAVE IT ALL FOR THE *ONE* THING THAT MEANS *ANYTHING.* LIKE *I* DID.

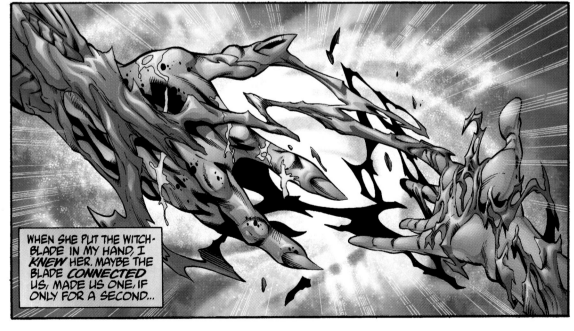

WHEN SHE PUT THE *WITCH-BLADE* IN MY HAND, I *KNEW* HER. MAYBE THE BLADE *CONNECTED* US, MADE US ONE, IF ONLY FOR A SECOND...

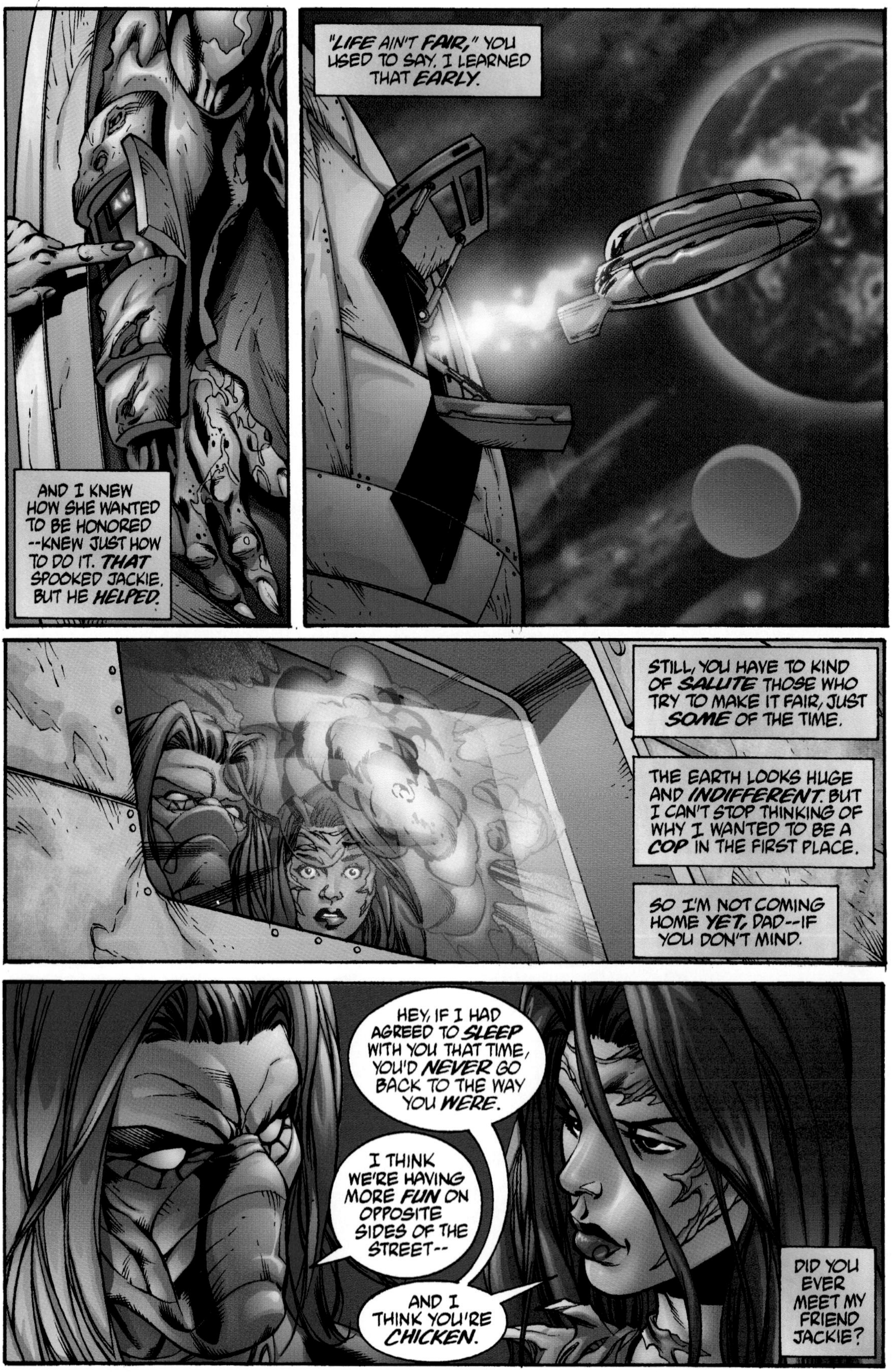
AND I KNEW HOW SHE WANTED TO BE HONORED --KNEW JUST HOW TO DO IT. THAT SPOOKED JACKIE. BUT HE HELPED.
"LIFE AIN'T FAIR," YOU USED TO SAY. I LEARNED THAT EARLY.
STILL, YOU HAVE TO KIND OF SALUTE THOSE WHO TRY TO MAKE IT FAIR, JUST SOME OF THE TIME.
THE EARTH LOOKS HUGE AND INDIFFERENT. BUT I CAN'T STOP THINKING OF WHY I WANTED TO BE A COP IN THE FIRST PLACE.
SO I'M NOT COMING HOME YET, DAD--IF YOU DON'T MIND.
HEY, IF I HAD AGREED TO SLEEP WITH YOU THAT TIME, YOU'D NEVER GO BACK TO THE WAY YOU WERE.
I THINK WE'RE HAVING MORE FUN ON OPPOSITE SIDES OF THE STREET--
AND I THINK YOU'RE CHICKEN.
DID YOU EVER MEET MY FRIEND JACKIE?

FIN

COVER GALLERY

ORIGINAL SERIES COVERS BY DWAYNE TURNER

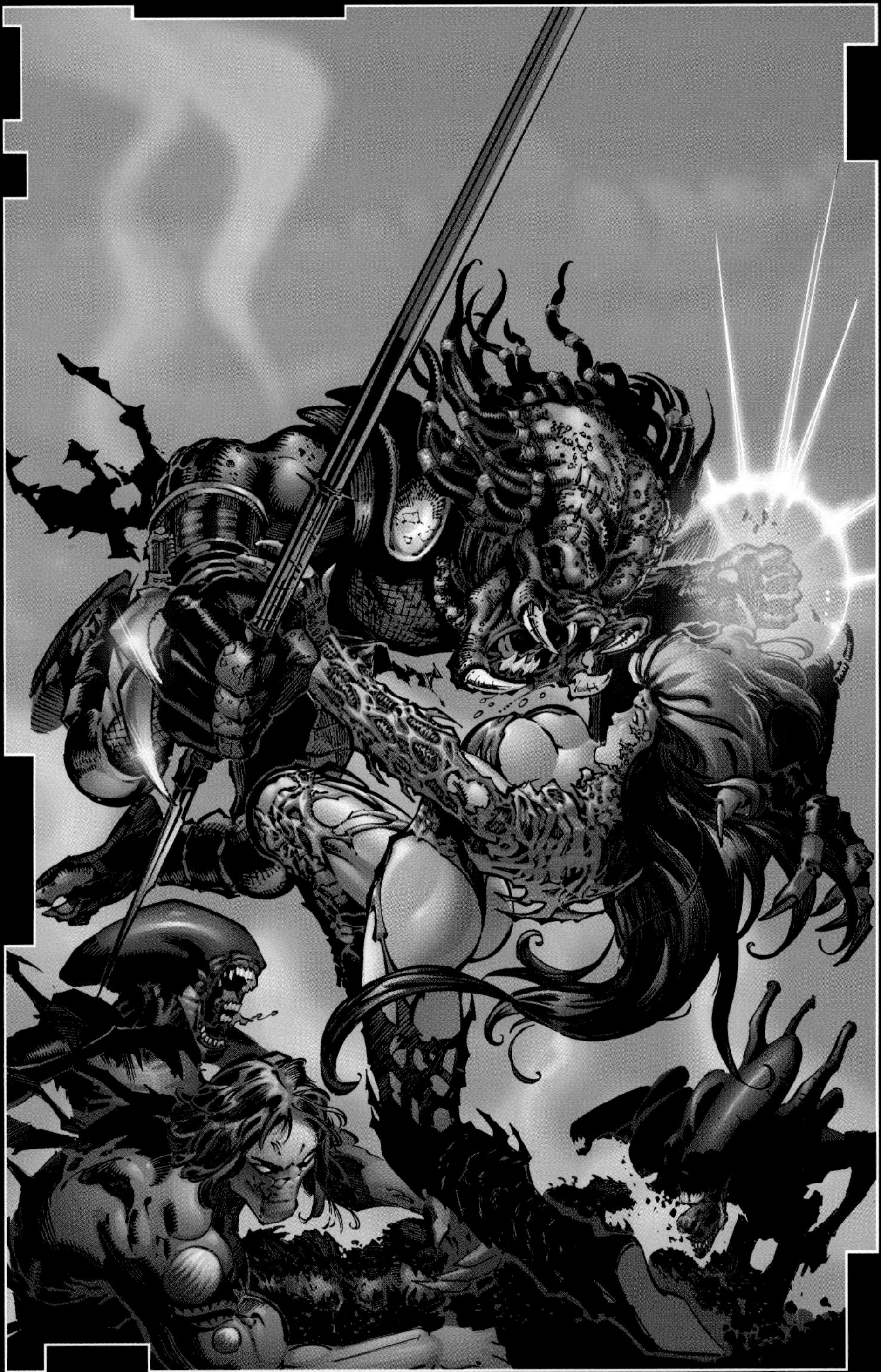

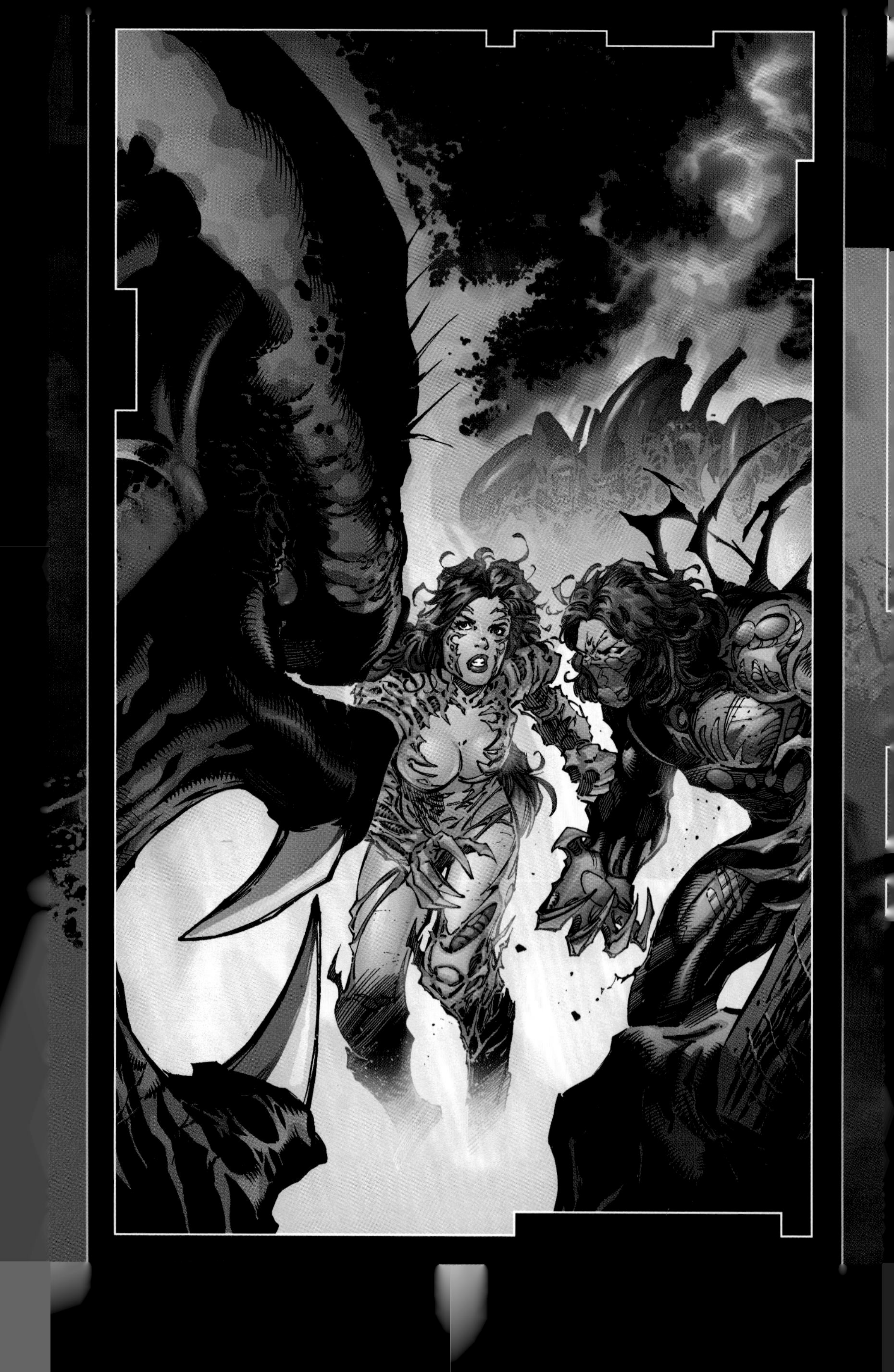

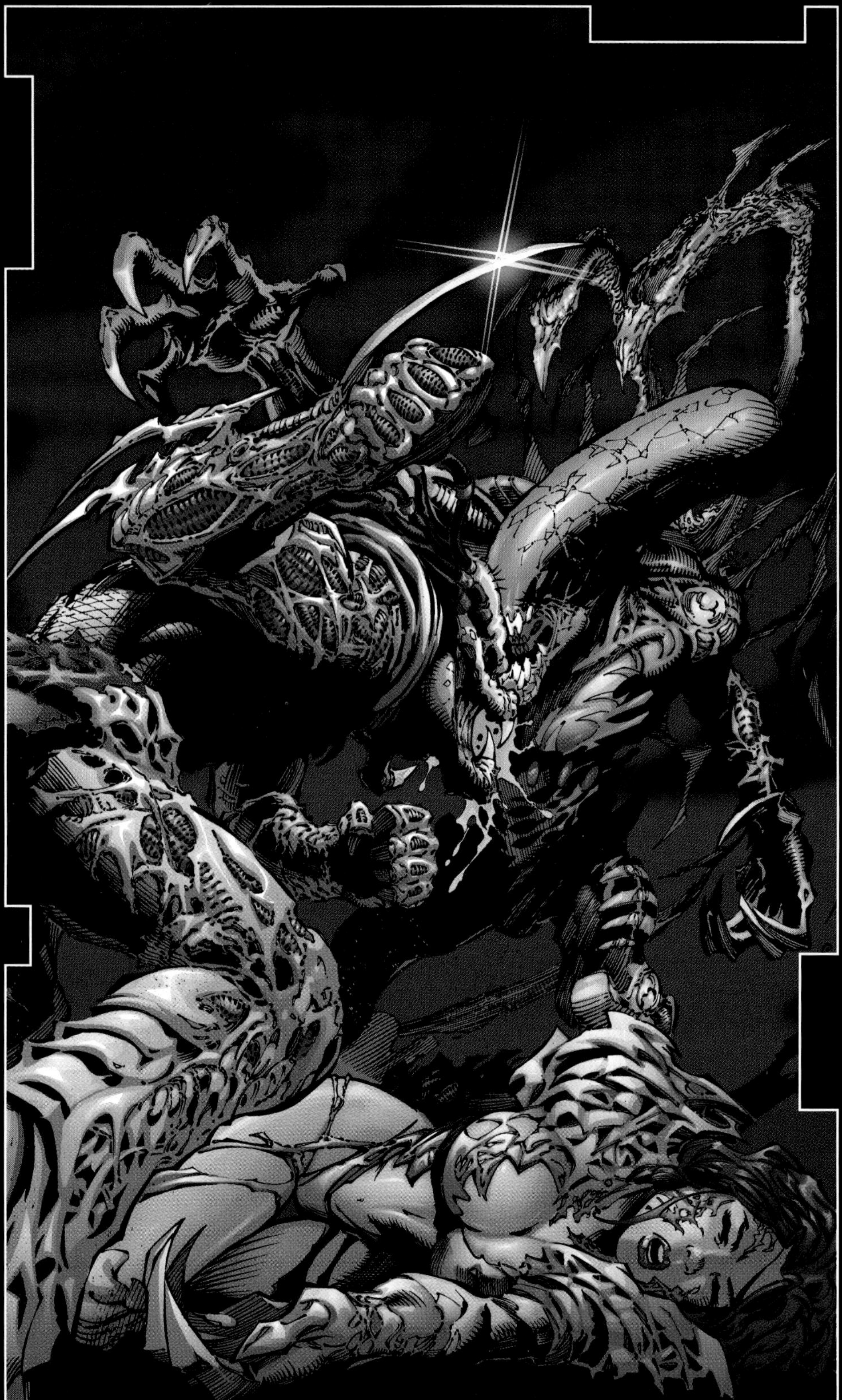

SKETCH GALLERY

ORIGINAL COVER SKETCHES BY ERIC KOHLER
PENCILS BY MEL RUBI

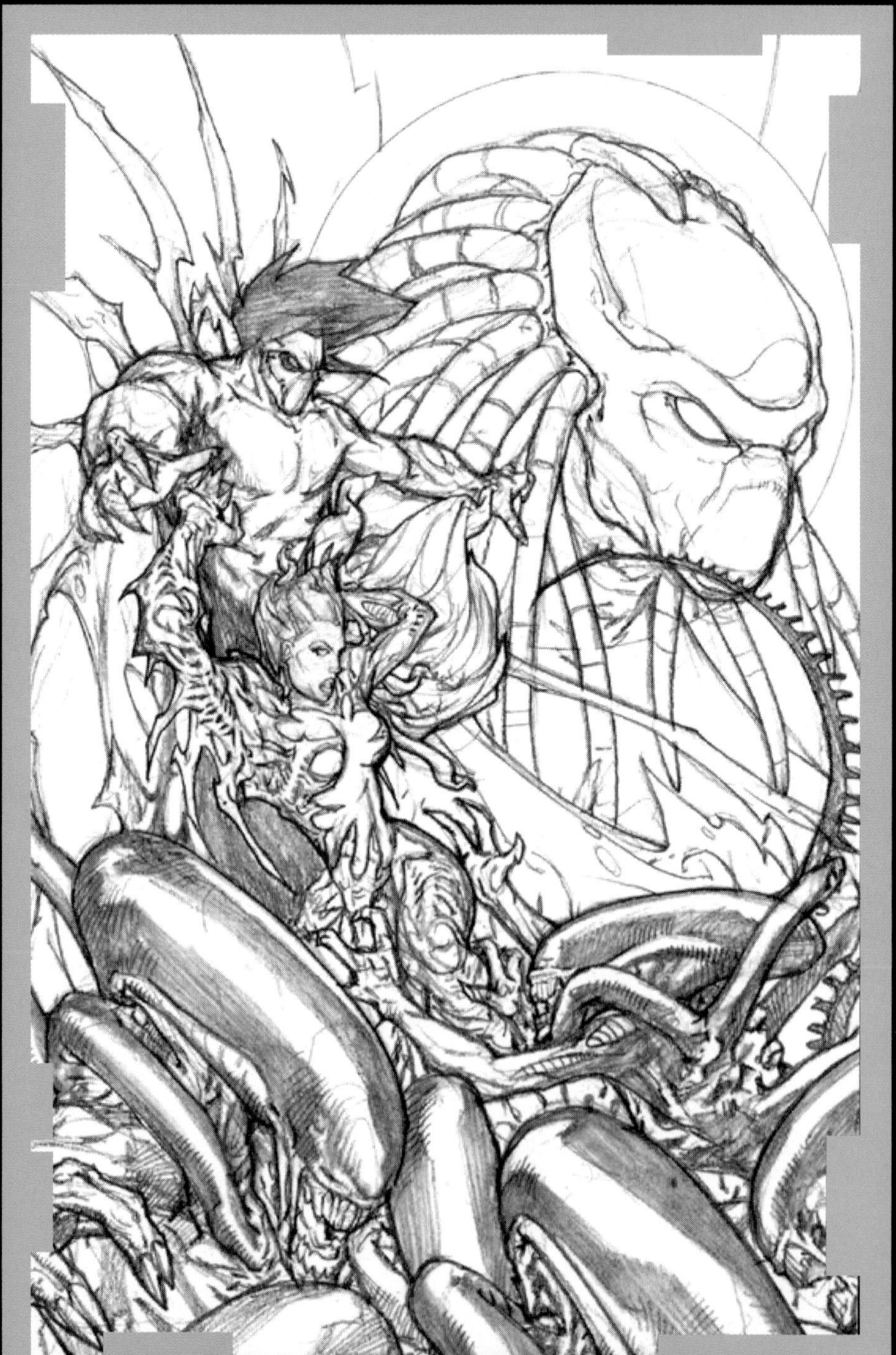

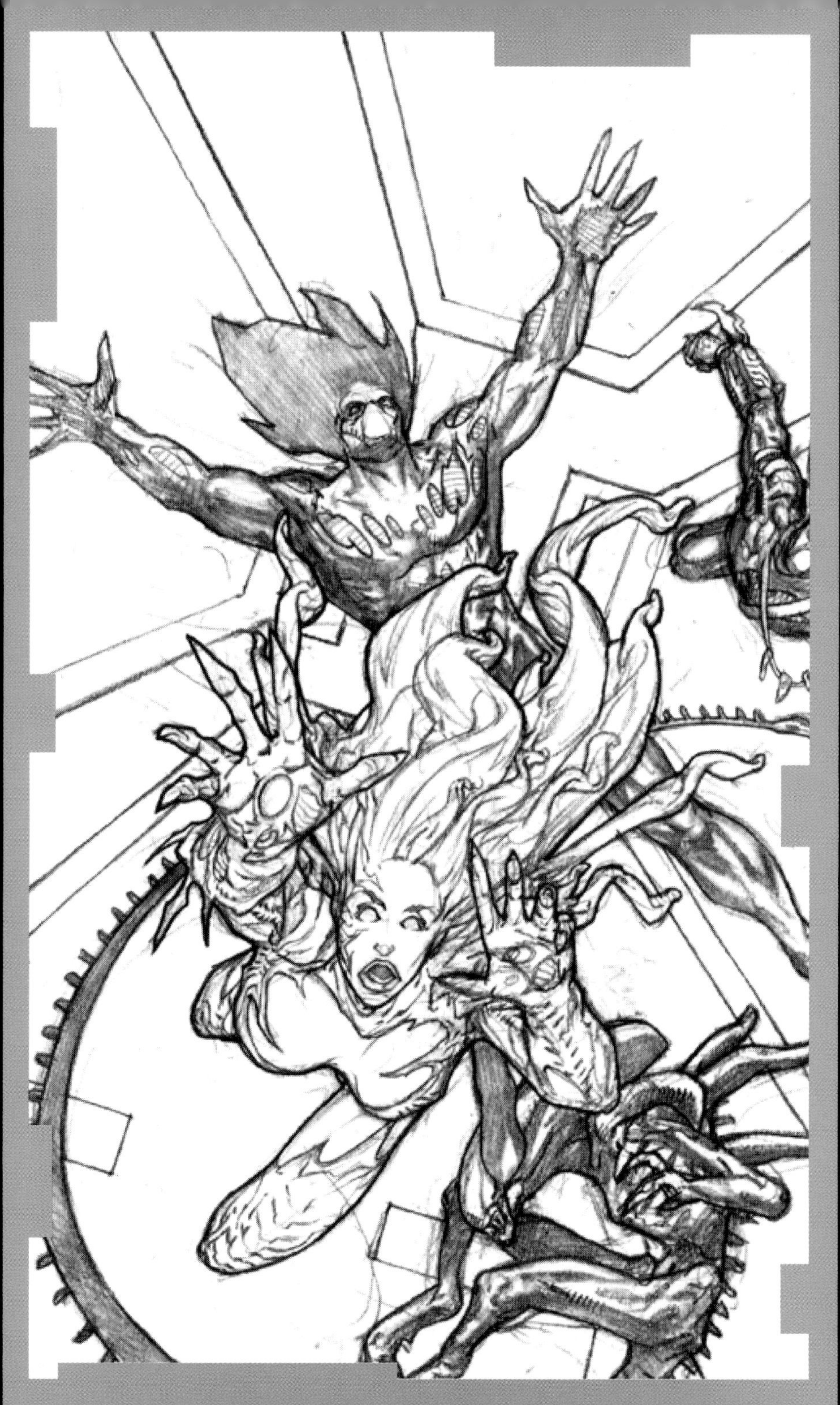

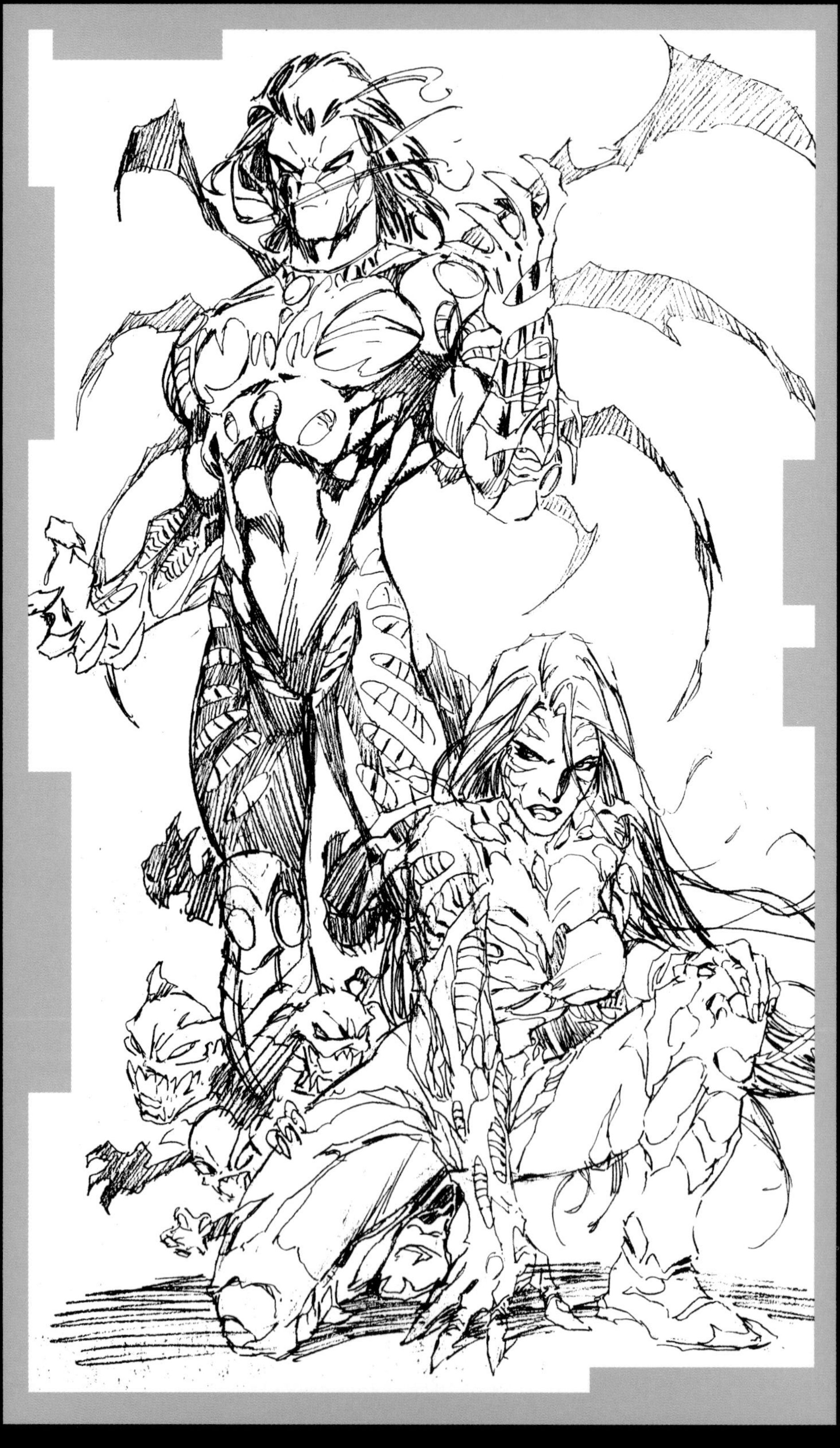

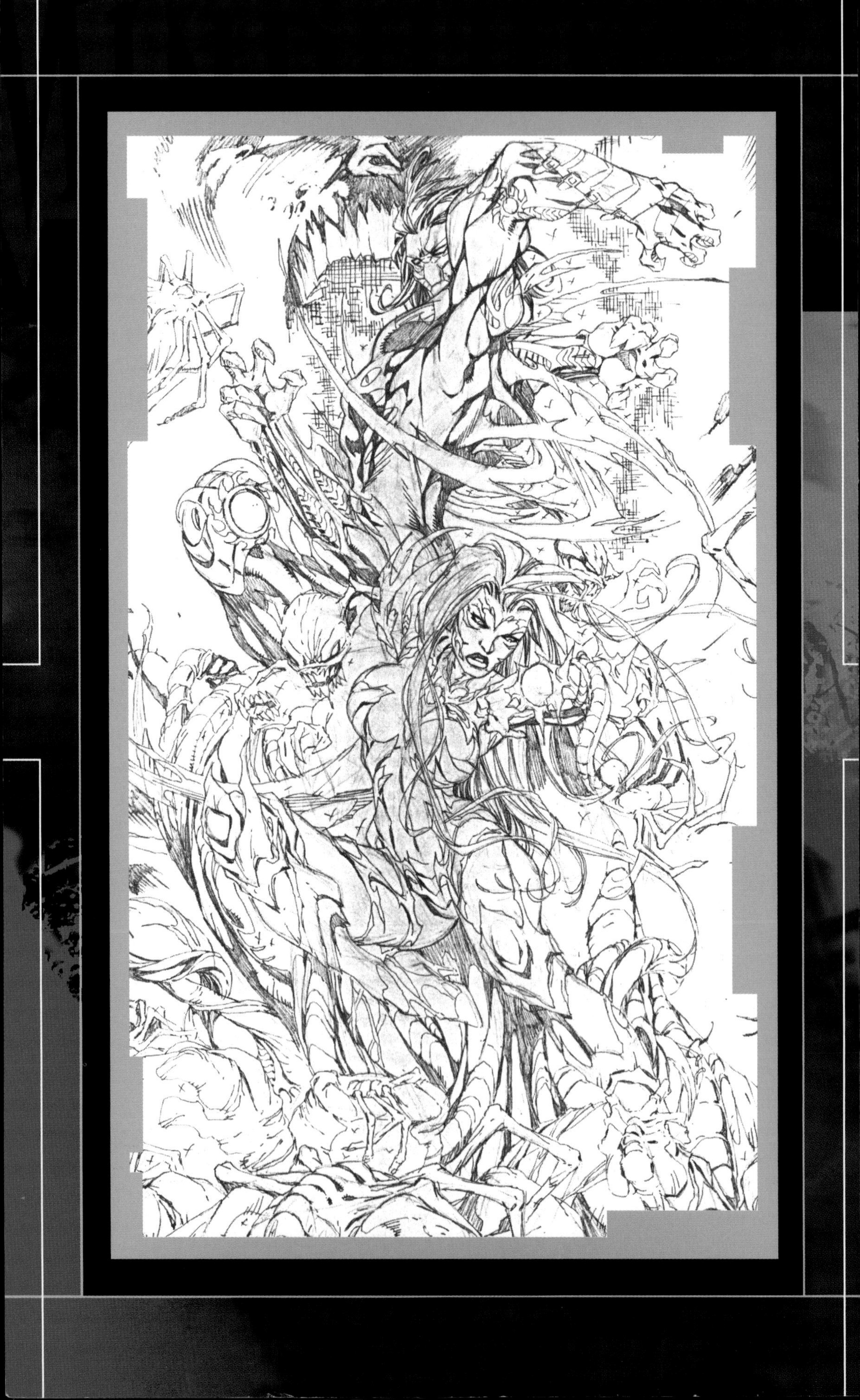

CREATORS

DAVID QUINN has contributed scripts to nearly every comics publisher, including Marvel, Image, DC, Chaos, and Avatar, though he's best known for his own creations, such as *Faust*, with long-time collaborator Tim Vigil. Quinn constantly showcases his versatility on mainstream action comics, horror comics, and his Not-for-Children children's book, *The Thirteen Days of Christmas*. Quinn's two-year run on Marvel's *Dr. Strange* in the early 1990s featured the first professionally published work of his *Mindhunter* collaborator, Mel Rubi.

MEL RUBI is one of the brightest newcomers in the Dark Horse stable of artists. Influenced strongly by both manga/anime and the horror work of artists such as Bernie Wrightson, Rubi blends the two styles seamlessly into his comics work. His Dark Horse Comics resume includes *Predator Xenogenesis, The Terminator*, the *Aliens vs. Predator Annual*, and *Aliens vs. Predator vs. The Terminator*. He is one of Dark Horse's most prolific and passionate creators, elements he will no doubt bring to the new *Angel* series, written by Joss Whedon.

MIKE PERKINS has worked as a penciller and inker on *Judge Dredd*, *Predator*, *Superman vs. The Terminator* with Steve Pugh, *Green Lantern vs. Aliens* over Rick Leonardi, and many others. He is a "smashing bloke," which means he's a nice guy, not a guy hired to break things. His career as an inker has taken him from the foggy, urban wilds of Birmingham, England to the sunny, humid wonderland that is Tampa, Florida.